My World of Cotton and Insects

Emotions in America, The Middle East, Far East and Africa

Pieter Stam

ARCHWAY PUBLISHING

Archway Publishing books may be ordered through booksellers or by contacting:

Archway Publishing
1663 Liberty Drive
Bloomington, IN 47403
www.archwaypublishing.com
1 (888) 242-5904

ISBN: 978-1-4808-7570-8 (sc)
ISBN: 978-1-4808-7569-2 (e)

Library of Congress Control Number: 2019902926

Print information available on the last page.

Archway Publishing rev. date: 6/18/2019

Foreword

This work is dedicated to my professors at the Louisiana State University

Kleverskerke, the Netherlands, January 2019

Acknowledgements

Many people have been important to me during my years in America. There are the professors at Louisiana State University (LSU), especially Dr. Dale Newsom, the head of the department entomology and my major professor for my PhD study; who by his example, and encouragement, showed me the way to learning. Dr Sess Hensley, sugarcane entomologist, a hard boiled taskmaster, but who also gave moral encouragement, when the going was difficult in Africa. Dr Dan Clower my major professor for my master study, always there to lend an ear and give advice. And then Dr Prentis Shilling, a statistics professor, who was always willing to explain a problem, even late at night in the department. With fond memory the friendship and hospitality of Dr.Joe Polack and his wife Anne. All of them passed away since but their memory will always remain with me. I will also not forget the friendship received of the family of Dr. Willem Kampen and the warmhearted Mrs A. Newsom, when the boss took his students home for a meal. All these amicabilities made a harsh study regime more enjoyable. And then there are the many colleagues I worked with at the FAO, in Syria, Turkey, Pakistan, the Sudan and at the university of Wageningen. The interaction with them was important and enriched my life. Last but not least my wife Gerda Stam-Poortvliet, who, under difficult living conditions created a home away from home in the Sudan and was an example for the people around her. Corrections to the English text were made by Mrs. Vanessa van Zijl.

Contents

Introduction

When writing a report or a scientific paper it is important that the material presented is concise and to the point. The emotion and hardship faced during the period the study took place are irrelevant and should not be mentioned. This booklet has been written with special attention to the emotions behind the exertion. For the person concerned the effort made is often more important than the actual results. So when there is time to reflect on one's past life and the decisions made, it is good to look back and speculate whether or not one could have decided differently at the time and what would have been the outcome of one's path in life!

Getting to know America

America, land of the free and unrestricted possibilities; I have always been interested and curious about the US of A. To get to know this country, which plays such an important role in the global happenings of the world. Experiencing it may give you more insight in the reasons for certain actions it undertakes.

I have finished my contract with Ciba Agrochemicals in Indonesia and now is the time to realize all my plans. Pieter, my boy what will yet happen to you in the future, I think in the airplane from Djakarta to Singapore, the first leg of my travel to America. I have taken my destination in my own hands. I now know exactly what I want to do.

During my work with Ciba Agrochemicals in Indonesia I became intrigued by the importance of insects and the damage they could inflict on an agricultural crop; in this instance rice. I witnessed the attack on 10.000 ha by a plant hopper (*Nilapervata lugens*). We could save the harvest by spraying a fumigant by plane, This experience really made me decide to learn more about the insect world and how to protect an agricultural crop from insect pests.

My travels through the USA will start in Hawaii, then to California, Arizona, Texas, Louisiana, Florida, New York and finally home, the Netherlands.

I am going to visit several old friends, student buddies

from the State College of Tropical Agriculture (RHSvTL), Deventer, the Netherlands. Rick and Jan are working in Hawaii and California respectively and have given me some good tips on how to prepare for studying in America.

Studying in America

The American university system consists of three levels; Bachelor of Science (BS) (*the Dutch higher technical school level (Ing)*, Master of Science (MSc), (*the Dutch university degree (Ir)* and Doctor of Philosophy (PhD), (*the Dutch Dr. title)*. The BS degree takes four years, a MS, two years and a PhD, two to three years, depending on the research project. For a MS degree a complete thesis research is required as well. Each year is split in semesters: spring semester, January – April ; summer term, May – August; winter semester, September – December.

I have decided to study Entomology and there are many universities to choose from. Professors and departments are truly excellent at certain research disciplines and it therefore advisable that you decide beforehand on your field of specialty and under which professor you want to study and do research. Some universities are renown. The University of California, with its campuses at Berkley, Davis and Riverside, has an excellent reputation. Then there is Cornell at the East coast and Texas A&M in the South, but there are others still and moreover the professor and his research are most important when making a choice. I have a few places in mind; California, Hawaii, Texas and Louisiana, a first selection made based on climate and agricultural research. So my travels and visits are planned accordingly.

Hawaii (1971)

It is a pleasure to meet up with Rick. He has continued his studies at the University of Hawaii and is now working on that beautiful island. Together we visit the university and I soon feel that I should not continue my education there to realize my objective.

The University of Hawaij does not have a Department of Entomology and moreover their graduate school is very conceited. My BS degree from Deventer is just not good enough for their school. The advice is; to first obtain a BS degree at their university. Rick counsels me not to accept this advice: 'You are much too good for this bull shit man. For me it was necessary because I did not study in Deventer, but you really worked there'.

I phone the sister of an acquaintance from Djakarta with the news that I have a nice present for her from her brother in Indonesia. She sounds enthusiastic and tells me that her husband will meet me at my hotel at 5.00 o'clock in the afternoon. I have to chuckle when I observe the curious looks of hotel personnel. Yesterday I was picked up by the Ciba representative in his big American car. Now another expensive car is waiting at the entrance, with a distinguished gentleman behind the wheel, Mr Tomson, the husband of the sister Mirna. The man does not say much, only looks and I get the impression that I'm being judged. We leave Honolulu and after fifteen minutes I see on the left their large ranch style house. I meet Mirna and her two children and hand over the big gift box. Mirna is trilled, she is really a beautiful woman with an enormous vitality. Dave is less enthusiastic and I cannot blame him.

During the evening meal I get to know Dave better and we get on well. He is the director of an American cargo business and he tells me how he had to explain the container business to the Japanese; instructions head office. He has been a sailor for many years and is really a very nice and interesting person. In the evening, not too late because next morning he has to get up early, he brings me back to my hotel.

Dave and Mirna invite me to see an exhibition the day after followed by dinner. When I mention Rick, with whom I had already indifferent plans., he is invited to join us, because Mirna is hospitable and likes to be surrounded by people. It is a nice evening my last in Hawaii, because the next day I shall fly to San Fransisco. I say goodbye to Rick, who in this short time has become a friend. Shall we meet again?

California (1971)

Arrival San Fransisco, 6.00 o'clock in the evening. I take the bus to the centre of town and check in at a small hotel, where you can rent a room by the hour and pay US$ 13 for the night. Rick gave me the address of a former RHSvTL student, who lives in Livermore, a certain Dick S. It is Saturday morning. I phone his number and when I introduce myself as a RHSvTL alumni, he knows enough. 'Where do you stay, please wait in the lounge, I will be with you in half an hour and you stay with us'. I am really flabbergasted; it is really a privilege to encounter so much hospitality. A small man enters the lounge, looks around and then asks me if I'm the student from Deventer. We shake hands and are on our way to Livermore.

It turns out to be a very nice weekend and I feel immediately at home with Dick and Liza his wife. When Dick graduated in Deventer, he emigrated to America and continued his studies there. Now he works already years for a technical firm in Livermore. He has the addresses of other former students of the RHSvTL, where I shall be very welcome; the good old network of Deventer students. I continue my travels. There is a farewell to two very nice people and then I'am on my way by Greyhound bus to Davis, where I want to visit the campus of the University of California. In Davis I meet Kees P., who obtained his MS at this university and now works there. That evening I'am sitting in my hotel room. I intend to visit the local cinema, because there is a movie, which I like to see. There is a knock on my door and when I open it I'm confronted with Kees and Ernst v Z., the older brother of an old student friend of mine. When I was a freshman at the RHSvTL fraternity, Ernst was a much older student. He had to leave Indonesia in 1957, lived in Deventer for a while, and then emigrated to America in 1958. He was at that time for us young people a very important person to whom you listened awestruck when he talked. And now this icon of my first student years is standing there just for me; inviting me to have dinner with him and Kees.

I stammer, completely overwhelmed by this unexpected sign of interest in wee me, that I intend to go to the cinema. Ernst curses something fiercely and then says 'Damn it, what do you want; go to the cinema or join us for a nice meal, you sapsucker'? I have recovered my wits and can think clearly again. 'Of course I come with you men, very nice of you to think of me, I did not expect this at all'! Ernst looks at me, shakes his head, mutters something like "stubborn", "drift-wood" and then says that I can stay with him and his family the coming weekend. When sitting next to Ernst in his car on the way to his home, I unwrap a piece of chewing gum and throw the paper out of the window. I receive then my first lesson in environmental protection, never to be forgotten, because the barrack language used by Ernst is something to behold.

I continue my travel and visit John K., an old student mate, who lives and works with his family in the San Jaquin valley. Jan works for a local company in seed production and they live in a small town in the middle of a large expanse of agricultural fields. They have to take it easy because the job does not pay very well; but John is an optimist and a fighter and is again full of plans. I have much respect for John and

I am also grateful to him, because he gave me really good advice on studying in America. 'Hé Piet, I have also the address of Bob K.. He lives in Riverside, nearby Los Angeles and has a job at the university there'. Well that is good news, because the campus Riverside of the University of California is on my list of universities in which I am interested. I locate Bob in the soils laboratory and he almost falls of his chair when I shout the old student RHSvTL rebel yell, I am hugged almost to death 'What are you doing here man, how long do you plan to stay. Yvonne will want to meet you'. Yvonne was already his girlfriend way back in Deventer. She is a nice, strong woman, who is in charge of this family of hers. She has recently opened a small restaurant in down town Los Angeles, which is doing well. Next morning Bob and I go there to help Yvonne and to wait for our old RHSvTL buddy Des Z., who shall arrive from Fresno by Greyhound bus.

Three old students, who started in year 1957, together again. We spend a very nice nostalgic evening. Yvonne is an excellent cook and after the meal we have permission to explore Los Angeles, under Bob's guidance, in good old Deventer style.

Louisiana (1971)

My expedition continues. Travelling by Greyhound bus I get to know America. People are getting in and out, impressions; the drifter who asking for money, the black dandy, who tries to intimidate me., the hippie girl in the bus, throwing me a skeptical look. And at the Riverside Campus that snobbish rich girl with her Mercedes Coupé, giving a fellow student, who just wants to chat a haughty turn down. All sorts of things that left a lasting impression.

I visit the universities of Arizona, Texas A&M, Louisiana and Florida, stay in motels and talk to professors. I'm notably impressed by Louisiana. At 10.00 o'clock in the evening I arrive in down town Baton Rouge. The streets are deserted. I start walking and see three men down the road. I call out to them, but they stay at a distance. They visibly relax when I ask for directions to a hotel and soon I'm standing in the lounge of down town hotel Baton Rouge.

The next morning I walk the three km to the university. It is a large campus with many trees and reminds me of Indonesia and makes me feel at home. I locate the Department of Entomology, which is housed on the third and fourth floor of the large Life Science building. An administrative assistant refers me to a certain Dr. Burns. At this time I'm still a quite heavy smoker and when we are talking I light a cigarette. The professor just looks at me but does not comment. Next I have a meeting with another professor, Dr, Graves, who does not say much but observes me with a certain curiosity. Much later, once we got to know each other better, he told me of their first impression of me: That strange dude with his short haircut, Dutch accent, and general appearance of this person from far away with his frequent smokes. When talking to Dr. Graves the door opens and a man enters, who introduces himself as Dr. Newsom, the head professor of the department. He asks me to pass by his office after lunch. When he learns that Dr Burns intends to show me around the experiment station, he nods in approval.

This meeting with Dr Newsom will turn out to be a very important one, and a turning point for me. He is truly interested in both my working experience in Indonesia and my goals and he lets me know that he would really like to take me on as his student. 'Where do you stay' he asks me. 'Tomorrow morning I am going to call on you and then I show you something of the university and what our Department of Entomology has to offer'.

In the afternoon, driving in a truck with Dr Burns and his assistant Danny, I am introduced to that comforter of the Louisiana farmer; *Red Man Chewing Tobacco*. Danny, a young big guy, does not say much, because with a dot *Red Man* in your mouth talking is somewhat difficult. However he is not stingy and he offers me generously a chew *Red Man* as being "something I have to try", claiming It's the best of the best. Of course I accept this generous offer and start to chew vigorously and that has its consequences. I swallow much tobacco juice, which results in a tremendous hick-up session, to the delight of the two Southerners. So another lesson learned; don't chew chewing tobacco, just keep it in your mouth and keep on spitting the juice; that 's really nice.

I learn that Louisiana has much to offer in the field of crop protection. Louisiana has a subtropical climate and grows cotton, soybeans, rice, maize and sugarcane; all of them crops in which I am very interested. Moreover, there is also a good chance to obtain a graduate assistantship, which makes it financially also very attractive. The environment reminds me of Indonesia, where I felt very much at home. But most important; Dr. Newsom impressed me more than any of the other people I have met so far. And that makes my decision to continue my studies in Louisiana a quick and simple one.

New York is my last stop before flying home to the Netherlands. I arrive in the morning but my connecting flight to Amsterdam leaves in the evening. So I take a bus to the city and walk around trying to understand this giant metropolis.

The Netherlands (1971)

It is always a pleasure to come home after a long period abroad and to stay with the parents in their nice and comfortable bungalow in Epse (Gorssel) The Netherlands. There is the period of rest and recuperation, certainly necessary after the exhausting time in Indonesia and America. I visit with friends and family and enjoy the lengthy conversations and the alcoholic beverages that accompany them.

To enter the graduate school of an American university you have to pass the Graduate Record Examination (GRE) and for a foreign student an English language test is mandatory as well. The GRE examination I take in Brussels and the language test in the Hague. During my stay in Louisiana I had the acute sence to buy a GRE training manual, which proofs very useful when studying for the exam at home. There is that nice daily routine when staying with my parents. First there's breakfast with father and mother. It is also nice for them to have one of the children at home again. It gives distraction and life in their very quiet existence as seniors. My days are structured around studies in the morning and in the afternoon I visit with friends or go for a run or help father in his garden. I also call on the Entomology Department at the University of Wageningen. Dr. de Wilde, the head of the department, is an impressive man who reminds me of my father. He is very friendly and suggests that I become one of his students, but he understands my fascination for studying in America.

Then there is good news from the LSU graduate school. I have passed the GRE examination and I'm accepted as a graduate student at their Department of Entomology. I can enroll the spring semester of 1972. Well that is something to look forward to. There is again purpose in my life, a new challenge. But first there is Christmas and New Year Eve, and all the preparations for a prolonged stay in the USA. I receive a nice letter from Dr. Newsom and for that first semester I file a request for student accommodation on campus.

And then there are the dates and talks with the girlfriend., who lives and works in Amsterdam. I met her when I was a student in Deventer, but we were not an item then. Karen is a very nice stately girl but I'm not certain if she is the right one for me. A holiday together on the island of Ameland is not a success. We are very different but there is the wish for stability in my life, especially now that I'm on the brink of a new challenge, possibly the toughest one yet. We agree to stay in touch, and time will tell if our liaison proofs lasting.

It's early January 1972 when I say goodbye to the parents. Our farewell at the Devener railway station is emotional. I see tears in the eyes of my father. It is hard for him to see this son depart by himself for an unknown future. I shall travel to Amsterdam by train,spend the night at my girlfriend Karen's place, and then the next morning she will take me to the square in front of the Rijksmuseum, and its bus stop for Schiphol Airport. From there I shall fly to my final destination; Baton Rouge Louisiana. In the plane I smoke my last cigarette, because I know that study and cigarettes don't work for me. In Louisiana I shall smoke pipe. My luggage consists of a briefcase and a suitcase. I have sent a very large suitcase as unaccompanied luggage.

Louisiana – LSU (1972)

Upon arrival at the Baton Rouge airport I take a taxi to the university and report to the office of the graduate school; I am expected. My initial request for a single room student accommodation on campus is not being approved. Which is not without reasons. They have experience in lodging foreign students, and they have put in place special arrangements. There is a dormitory solely used by older graduate students and foreigners. Two students to a room much better indeed; this way newcomers will get to know fellow students, avoiding the risk of isolation and loneliness. During my first semester in that dormitory I make several friends for life. There is Jim, he has a rice farm in Louisiana, 41 years old and studying poultry science. When my unaccompanied luggage arrives he instantly offers to help and collect the suitcase together in his pick-up truck. We drink together our first cup of café in the student union and several times I stay with him and his family at his farm in the rice fields of Louisiana. Then there is Shelley from Mississippi, a very warm and gentle person, who studies for his MBA. He is very much in love with a girl back home, but is not sure if she does want to marry him or not; there is this darn other fellow! So I encourage him, mention his tremendous sex appeal, his pluck studying for a degree in administration in order to increase his prospects for a good job in the future, and so on. My roommate Pete is a Vietnam veteran, from Iowa. He has a BS in forestry. He confides in me that his mean reason to continue his studies is to meet nice Southern girl. When in Vietnam, he received a *"Dear John"* letter from his then girlfriend, in which she wrote him that she wanted to end their engagement. Fortunately for him he had a rest and recreation (R&R) leave coming up in Hong Kong, where he met some nice girls, who put his "loss in love" in perspective again. Big Allen from Alabama, studies Social Sciences, and is already convinced that he will never meet a girl who will fall for him, because he is too fat.

Yes we students on the first floor of building C form a kind of a family. We study completely different disciplines, but we drink our café together, take our meals in the giant student cafeteria and talk about our daily experiences. It gives us a feeling of belonging. Sometimes there are funny situations. Ray, the chemistry major, likes his girls. One evening when I'm in de communal bathroom, Ray comes in and asks if I can wait a few minutes because his present girl is in high need. Yes, girls are always welcome on our floor, although I keep myself far from this distraction. One evening, when I'm sitting in my room studying, I receive a telephone call. A few girls are trying to talk to me. They have learned that I'm a foreign student and they want to know if I like boobies. When I tell them that I'm an elderly student and have to study very hard, there is silence on the other end of the line, after which a more mature girl takes over. She introduces herself with the family name of a Louisiana senator in Washington and apologizes for their call. No hard feelings, I assure her, I kind of liked the exchange but I have my priorities.

At the faculty I share a room with a post graduate fellow, Dr. Chen W.. He's from Indian descend, graduated a few years ago and completed a very fine study on the banded-wing whitefly (*Bemisia trialorodus*). He is looking for a job but works in the meantime for his and also my major professor Dr. Dan Clower., who is in charge of the cotton insect research program. We soon form a team and I often have to assist Chen in his work for Dr. Dan. We travel then by truck to one of the research stations - Red River or St Joseph - to carry out observations in one of the experiments of Dr. Dan's research program. We spend the night in a motel and return to the university the next day. Dr. Dan is continuously testing the efficacy of new insecticides for cotton-related insect pests.

During the day I attend lectures and in my so called "free time" I study, and study, and study some more. The interludes assisting Dr. Chen or Dr. Dan are in fact very useful and healthy intervals in my study agenda, although I am not too happy with any field trips that interrupt an intense study session. No, on a daily basis my main occupation is to study, period. And at night there's more of the same," burning the midnight oil" as they call it. For graduate students, the required scholastic average after each term is at least a B. An average of C or D means you are in trouble, and you are not allowed to continue graduate school. Still, I enjoy it, because I learn much and make progress. One subject, which apart from the entomology curriculum, really fascinates me are the statistics classes. The importance of this subject I learned during my work in Indonesia. It is an important tool in the biological sciences to evaluate the differences between insect populations and to compare harvest results in different fields. Therefore, during that first semester in 1972 I enroll in the first graduate statistics course, together with first courses in entomology. My teacher is Dr.Prentice Shilling., a professor in the department, an excellent teacher and always willing to explain a certain problem to me. Often he is still late at work in the statistics department, where I then go to see him when I am desperate. Then there are the exams, the hours of preparation, the hour X of upper concentration, "top sport". And then the hour after, to unwind in the student union with fellow students.

Yes that first semester is a pressure cooker, but when it is over I have a B average. I feel pretty good to have taken this first o so important huddle. Dr. Dan, my major professor, congratulates me with this result. He is happy that his student has made the grade.

Cotton in Louisiana

During 1972 and 1973 an average of about 600.000 acres was planted in cotton in Louisiana. There are three insect pests that are of major importance; the boll weevil (*Anthonomus grandis*) a beetle, which feeds on buds and flowers, the cotton bollworm (*Helicoverpa zea*), feeding on buds, flowers and bolls, and the banded-wing whitefly (*Trialeurodes abutilonea*). The immature and adult specimen of the latter are almost entirely confined to the underside of leaves. They damage the plant through direct feeding and by producing honeydew, causing the growth of sooty mold on plant parts and lint, the latter getting sticky and off color. The white fly is basically a secondary pest, which erupts after excessive use of insecticides decimating predators and parasites.

Thesis research

Then it is summer; the period of my thesis "field research", an important requirement for a MS degree. Dr. Dan has a nice research project in store for me. When farmers have their cotton sprayed with herbicides by airplane, it is observed that many beneficial insects are being killed. So Dr. Dan's objective: to find out if the herbicides used are toxic to insects too.

Thesis: *Effects of certain herbicides on some arthropod populations occurring in cotton in Louisiana(1)* Experiments were conducted at the Northeast Louisiana Experiment Station during the summer of 1972 and at the Red River Valley Experiment Station in 1973. The objective was to determine whether some widely used herbicides had a detrimental effect on the arthropod fauna in cotton fields and if so, whether changed methods of application could alter that effect. Furthermore, bioassays on several major beneficial insect species using these herbicides were conducted in the laboratory, and LD50's were established.

Field work

Spring semester is over, and for the time being classes are finished, so it is time for some work in the fields. Dr. Dan wants me to work at the NE. Experimental Station that first summer, located near the small town St Joseph, close to the Mississippi river. On a beautiful morning in April '72, Dr. Dan picks me up at my dormitory in a university truck and together we drive to St Joseph. There I am introduced to the station's permanent staff, notably the chief agronomist, Mr. Leonard S., who will supervise my fieldwork. Mr. .Leonard shows us several fields planted in cotton, where I can lay out my experiments and then it is up to me. The research proposal I developed was approved by Dr. Dan, and it is a pleasure to lay out the plots, and walk the fields. I make observations in each plot before and after an application of a herbicide, which is sprayed on by a tractor-driven rig. I have rented a room in a neighboring motel, but in the evenings I go back to the station to count the insects collected in the samples. It's anything but easy. I am sleepy after a day in the field and a nice hot meal in the evening. On Mondays I drive to the station and then on Fridays I return to Baton Rouge and the university. One Friday I am out with Dr. Dan, assisting him at the St Joseph experiment station, carrying out observations in one of his insecticide screening experiments. That Saturday morning we drive back to Baton Rouge. When we approach town we see dark clouds forming and the streets are practically void of traffic. 'It looks like there's a hurricane coming', mutters Dr. Dan, and advices me to go home quickly when we have reached the university's parking lot where I have parked my Volkswagen Beetle. I am alone at home because my two roommates have gone home for the summer holidays. I am tired, go to bed early while a heavy rain pours down and I am soon fast asleep. The next day, Sunday morning, I want to go to the university church. It is unusually quiet with hardly any people out, but the streets are splayed by many tree branches from the gale of yesterday. When I arrive at the church there is nobody around and I take a seat in the empty pews. The vicar enters, throws me a surprised look, and then tells me today's service has been cancelled due to the last night's heavy gale.

University

That summer 1972 passes by rather quickly and I enjoy these months of sun and rain. Then fall semester starts, and it is again back to the grind of classes and study. Also there are still many glass jars with ethyl alcohol left whose insects need counting, a task I was unable to finish during the summer months. Then there are the endless hours in the library, conducting literature research for my thesis. So I am kept busy and completely obscured with life on campus. One day, during those first months of total absorption in study, I feel kind of other-worldly; driving to Baton Rouge seems suddenly a tremendous undertaking. It's a really strange feeling; me, who has travelled the world! The feeling passes, but it is an experience which I shall never forget. My work for Dr. Dan continues. In a greenhouse he grows cotton on which he maintains a population of whiteflies for lab studies. It is my responsibility to water the plants every day. One Saturday morning I find the door of the greenhouse locked. It's hot inside and the plants need water. I feel I have no choice but to break a window in order to open the door. On Monday morning I am sitting in my room with Dr. Chen, when an angry Dr.Dick Jensen., the assistant of Dr.Newsom comes barging in. We have a shouting match, since I am furious for being accosted by him in that manner. Dr. Newsom wants to see me and I have to explain why I damaged that window. 'You should have asked for a key from Dr. Dick or myself' he tells me. He understands my reasoning, but warns me against damaging university property again.

Field work

Summer 1973: Dr. Dan has moved his main research program to the Red River Valley Experiment Station near the town of Shreveport. Mr. Derrick M. is here the chief agronomist and the man to coordinate my work at his station. Together with Chen I make several trips to the station to lay out experimental plots for Dr. Dan's research program, including my work with herbicides. It is always fun to be on the road with Chen. We have our disagreements, because we are both kind of stubborn, but we work well together and I learn a lot about his specialty, the banded-wing white fly. Some evenings we visit a bar in the neighborhood. Quit often a few Air Force pilots from the nearby airbase are standing around and talk about their flights to Vietnam. We sit at the bar and sip our drinks. The lady behind the bar is somewhat older and very experienced in getting some life out of her customers. She starts talking about whores and more of those kind of tidbits, which really keep her male customers wide awake and the talk around her bar lively. Dr. Dan is rather disappointed when I decide not to continue a PhD cotton research program under his guidance. I explain that I feel that a change in crops will give me a wider expertise, the fundamental reason to switch universities in the first place. However I like him to remain one of my advisors. He understands my reasoning and there are no hard feelings.

Accommodations and Domestic Life

After three months in a dormitory I'm ready to find accommodation off campus; preferable a detached house. I am in love. She is a nice sturdy girl, a graduate student in the Department of Geography. Yes, Judy M. likes me, but she is still in love with her former boyfriend, much older then she and an associate professor at the University of South Carolina. Judy tells me that one of the students in her department has graduated and will be leaving LSU and Louisiana. He lives with his family in a cute little house South of campus and if I am quick it could be mine. Two student friends from dormitory C like to move in with me. Mark M. is a graduate student in the Department of Marine Biology and originally from Boston. Phil, a graduate student in Business Administration has his roots in rural Louisiana. Mark is a big fellow from Italian stock, an extrovert, who talks a blue mile with a ready smile under a big moustache. Phil is the opposite, a very shy person, who has no experience outside Louisiana and enjoys listening to Mark and me swapping stories.

It's a wooden house that has been neglected by its owner, a real slum lord, who prefers students lodgers since they're not too demanding. The house is located in a nice residential area with many trees. It has three bedrooms, a living room, a dining area and a kitchen, with a patch of grass surrounding the place. In April 1972, after furnishing the place, we move in. In a second hand store we buy a couch, two easy chairs and window curtains. Phil and me both buy beds, but Mark decides on a waterbed, which – obviously - tears a few months later flooding his room. A married student in my department has to buy a color TV for his wife and lets me have their old black and white one. After leasing a fridge and gas stove, we are in business. Phil is the only one who cooks; Mark and myself take our warm meals at noon in the student union; it is cheap, good and convenient. Breakfast and a cold supper we take at home. Mark and I furnish our own desks using wooden doors purchased at a "do it yourself" store. However after dinner and the TV news I often go to my room at the department to study, because at home I cannot focus with the others watching TV or entertaining friends. Phil and Mark are good housemates and we are getting on well. They both graduate in 1974 and leave LSU. Phil gets a job in Texas and Mark transfers to the University of California to study for a PhD degree.

A wooden house with deferred maintenance surrounded by a lawn, and moreover, a genuine student residence: It's heaven for all kinds of insects and we have our share of un-wanted occupants. Cockroaches, termites and fleas are un-wanted guests and cause embarrassing situations. At first our living room is adorned by a large rug on the floor. Not too expensive, mind you, since we could not afford any of that. One evening I have some guests over for drinks. I sit on our couch next to a nice lady. Suddenly I see her furtively rubbing her nice bare leg, not once but several times. And then I see some something shocking on the rug; fleas dancing a polka, close to the feet of my lady guest. That same evening I throw our rug out in the garden.

I finish my Masters study in the spring of 1974. I am not sure however whether I should continue my studies, and if so, if that would be at LSU or another university. The initial plan has always been to go back to work with a MS degree. One morning Dr. Newsom summons me to his office and shows me a telegram from Ciba Agrochemicals, my former employer in Indonesia. They congratulate me on my MS degree and there is an offer for a position as an entomologist for a project on mosquito control in Saudi Arabia. 'Well Piet what are you going to do' asks Dr. Newsom, 'continue your studies which I recommend or back to industry'?. I have already made up my mind to continue my studies for a PhD degree. However I want to explore the possibility of studying at the University of California, campus Davis, in their rice program. So, in April 1974 I drive in my VW beetle through Texas, Arizona, and New Mexico to Davis California, where I visit with the professor in charge of the insect pest control program on rice. He has a proposal for a research project, but I am not really excited about the problem. Moreover, studying at the University of California is expensive and the professor cannot offer me a graduate assistantship for the first six months. However he tells me that it might be possible to work for a colleague of his in the Weed Sciences Department. When I meet the man I know that I should not work for him; there is that gut-feeling that he will be very difficult to get along with. I decide not to continue my study at Davis. At LSU I can work in the soybean research program of Dr. Newsom on a research project which interests me. So I make up my mind to stay at LSU, and it feels like the right decision.

The Netherlands (1974)

In order to visit my family in the Netherlands I ask permission to be absent from the ceremony to receive my MS degree in December 1974. It is nice to be home again, the parents proud of my degree. Still they would like to see me settled. 'Well Piet what are you going to do now' my father asks? 'I strongly suggest you get back to work and find yourself a nice girl'. He looks at me expectantly, well aware that his advice has always been very important to me. But my mind has been made up long ago, and I know exactly what I need to do. So I reply my father; 'well next week I am going back to university and continue my study for a PhD degree'. My father does not reply, and just looks at me with a smile on his face. He realizes that this son of his has at long last grown up and knows what he wants to do. He is reassured; he does not have to worry about this son no more. Karen, the girl friend, says she wants to visit me in Louisiana, but I tell her that is not a good idea. I shall be very busy with study and doing research work so there will be hardly time to spend with her. Moreover, I am quite sure now that we have no future together. Karen does not like the tropics and I know that my way of life is not for her. 'Let's just remain friends, it will be better for both of us', I tell her. And then it's off to Louisiana, back to the grind.

University Louisiana (1975)

PhD research

Dr. Newsom has an interesting research project in mind for me. The Southern green stinkbug (*Nezara viridula*) is an important pest in Louisiana soybeans. The question is; which factors affect its development on soybeans?

Dissertation: Relation of Predators to Population Dynamics of *Nezara viridula* in a Soybean Ecosystem (2)(6)

In farmers fields observations were carried out during 1975, 1976 and 1977, with as major objectives to; a) determine the predators of *N. viridula* and define their relative importance, and b) to assess their quantitative impact on *N. viridula* population development in a soybean ecosystem.

Fieldwork

In America Dr. Newsom is a leading entomologist in America and well renowned for his work on IPM. Instead of using Experimental Stations, he prefers to work in actual farmers fields. He is an outdoors man, who really loves to be out in the field. At least once a week he leaves his office to investigate soybean fields all over Louisiana, inviting several of his students to join him. With ground-sweep nets we sample rows of soybean plants and count the insects caught directly in the field. You have to recognize various kinds of insects and larvae and to keep a mental tally of the numbers you caught. Once your sampling finished, you note the collected amounts for each species. We do not just sample soybean fields this way but the vegetation along roads and fields as well. It is hot thirsty work but our professor believes in water discipline for both himself and us. We of course want to prove that we can also discipline ourselves, but sometimes we cheat. During a lunch break we leave our mentor in the field with his lunch packet and bottle of water and take the truck to a hamburger stand in the nearest village, where we take hamburgers and coca cola. Back again it's always a pleasure to minutely explain to the boss the niceties of a cold coca cola and a juicy hamburger. His reaction; showing his still full bottle of water and his promise to work our bottoms off *"you good for nothings"*. Yes, our professor is a very bright and tough man, but he also cares about his students. He inspires us with his example and work ethics.

Angola prison farm: Louisiana has a penitentiary farm of about 1000 ha, that grows agricultural crops like cotton and soybeans. The prisoners work the fields, supervised by armed guards on horseback. Dr. Newsom likes to come to the Farm to research population dynamics of the Southern green stinkbug, a perfect place since its isolated location makes migration difficult. We students often assist him thereby. The prisoners are a rough bunch and their guards are a tough lot too. On the farm we sample wild vegetation and soybean fields, eyed curiously by prisoners and guards alike. Sometimes there is a longing cry *"white meat"* by one of the inmates, but they don't bother us. When one of the guards shows interest in our work, Dr. Newsom gives him a sweep net to that he can sample fields in his spare time.

In order to obtain a Doctor of Philosophy degree (PhD),

you are required to personally develop and oversee the planning, implementation and logistics of your research. Your major supervisor, in my case Dr. Newsom, will only observe, criticize and give occasionally encouragement, when the going gets real tough. You are just expected do it. Still, my professor cares about his students and knows when a pat on the back is needed. Often we are invited to his home, where Mrs. Newsom serves a lovely meal and then there is stimulating conversation and again the magic of realizing that we are engaged in something worthwhile.

It is April 1975, and I don't know where to start. I have written a research proposal, which has been approved by Dr. Newsom, but now I have to start the actual work. First I need to find a way to label nymphs (immatures) and adults of *N. viridula* with radio phosphorus (P32). The advice of Dr. Ned Lambremont. of the Nuclear Science department, whose course on working with radioisotopes I followed, is very helpful. Thoroughly washed tomatoes were injected with a 32P solution, fitted into a petri dish and then placed in a carton box containing the desired number of nymphs or adults. An average of 3 days feeding was required to obtain a satisfactory level of radioactivity. About 100 to 200 radioactive nymphal instars were released at one time in a soybean field. After three days ca. 45 meter row of soybean plants around the release point were sampled using ground cloth and sweep net, and the occasional pitfall trap. Predator insects and spiders were collected and placed in plastic bags, which contained some heptachlor 10% granules in order to kill them. Taken back to the laboratory, these were then assayed for radioactivity using the Cerenkov counting technique (6). An observation was recorded as positive when the insect's level of radioactivity measured was two times the background radiation.

That first positive result observed one evening is a

memorable occasion, a first breakthrough. I am really excited when I see the radiation level climb well above the background radiation. The next morning I inform Dr. Newsom of
this first result and he congratulates me. In the beginning he
was rather skeptical of this approach, but now we have results
to be proud of. However the best way to assess predation is
by direct observations in the field. In order to do this I glue
egg masses to leaves and release nymphal instars at certain
spots. Every hour I check each location and look if I can detect
predators feeding. It is tiring work, slogging through rows
of soybean plants. The reward is there however; observing
a direct interaction, a grasshopper feeding on an egg mass,
an ant feeding on a nymphal instar. I make then a photo of
such an incident and feel pretty good and reenergized. I walk
those fields in rain, wind and sunshine and wear out several
pairs of field shoes.

Social contacts

The department of foreign student affairs informs me
that there is another Dutchman studying at LSU. His name:
Willem K.. He and his family are living in a flat not too far
from my place. One Saturday morning I go there to meet
him. Willem is a big fellow, from Groningen. When he opens
the door there is an instant recognition and a welcom-
ing smile. I'm introduced to his wife and their two small
children. We share a lot of common ground; Willem is an
ex-sergeant in the Dutch Commando Corps, Pieter an ex in-
fantry sergeant in New Guinea. Willem studied at the Sugar
College in Amsterdam, Pieter at the RHSvTL Sugar College
in Deventer. Both of us have worked in the tropics; Willem
in Suriname, Pieter in Malaysia and Indonesia. Willem now
studies Chemical Engineering. We hit it off straight away. His
wife is an excellent cook, and they often invite me over for

dinner. We both play tennis and many a Saturday afternoon is spent on hard fought matches at an university tennis court with Willem-admittedly-often the victor.

One Saturday morning I am invited by Willem for drinks at their place. There I meet Dr. Joe P. and his wife Anne. Joe is the head of the Department of Chemical Engineering and also Willem's major professor. They are both really nice, and Joe tells Willem to bring me along next time he comes over for a meal. Those evenings by Joe and Anne, never to be forgotten. Willem would pass by my house and telling me 'Pieter we are invited for a meal by Joe and Anne. I shall pick you up a 6.00 pm tonight'. Quite often they had other guests over as well, and we enjoyed the excellent food and stimulating conversation on all kinds of subjects. One time we are told to dress up since we shall be meeting an important person. When we arrive at Joe and Anne, smartly dressed in jacket and tie, they introduce us to Dr. Eugene Wigner and his wife. Wigner, the Noble Price Winner in Physics 1963, works at the university for a while. We feel very privileged to share this occasion, that is only granted to a lucky few. There is stimulating conversation. Willem is very good at mathematics. He is not easily impressed, and has many searching questions for Dr. Wigner. I have not much to say, because mathematics and physics are not my strong suit. Joe does not say much either, He is smiling though, and enjoys the exchange between Willem and Dr . Wigner. Chuckling he informed us later that Dr Wigner told him that he was unable to sleep after talking to Willem; the exchange had made an impression on him. Willem graduates with a PhD in Food Science and gets a job with a large chemical company in New Jersey, and the family departs for a new life. I miss our weekly get-togethers, but we stay in touch. Occasionally business trips for his company bring him to Louisiana and then we meet up and often have dinner with Joe and Anne.

Graduation time (1978)

My graduation committee consists of six professors. Three of them are entomologists; Dr D. Newsom, my major professor, Dr. S. Hensley and Dr. D. Clower. Then there are Dr. K. Koonce, a statistics professor, Dr E. Lambremont, head of the Nuclear Science department, and Dr. L. Black, a plant pathologist.

I pass my final exam, the defense of my dissertation research, on 28 June 1978 and may call myself a Doctor in Philosophy (PhD). During an impressive graduate ceremony, during which all the graduates that semester receive their bull, the PhD graduates are called one by one to step forward to receive their bull from the President of the university. Then it is all over and I can relax. After the ceremony some friends congratulate me and also Dr. Newsom is there with a big smile to pound me on the back. With my good friend Shelley I go to a restaurant to celebrate this big day with a beer. Then Shelley has to go back to work and I drive back home. It is a beautiful sunny day. I have the house to myself, since Frank, my present house mate is staying with his girlfriend and from there will go directly to his family in Mississippi. I'm alone and there is a feeling of "let down" After so many years of study and work, the objective is reached and there is nothing left to do. I miss having friends and a social life. Well, Joe and

Anne invite me over to celebrate my graduation that night, but that's about it.

I have applied for a job with the FAO. There is a good chance that I can work for the organization in Syria. My actual appointment however has to be approved of by the Syrian government. I also apply for a job with a chemical company in Indiana and there is an invitation for an interview at their head office in Indianapolis. I call Willem and ask if I can visit with them coming from Indiana, thus cutting the combined flight charges in two.

The interview at the chemical company is a disappointment. Or more accurately, I'm rather amazed about their job offer. Their sales manager for South America is of Dutch origin. After a first cup of coffee and some small talk - it turns out he used to work in Hong Kong and we have some acquaintances in common - we are suddenly palls, and we talk business. The job offer is a position in Brazil. But as a non- American I shall be paid in the local currency and not in US Dollars. 'Yes, sorry but it is a company policy'. But then, he could take my local currency and convert it to US Dollars, no problem. I am truly amazed about this offer, which can hardly be called professional. However I decide not to comment and, to await the meeting with the director of the overseas division. When I ask this good man about payment in US Dollars and other benefits such as paid holidays in America or Europe, he gets kind of excited and I know that I am not going to work for his outfit. However it is a good experience and another plus; it pays for 50% of my air fare to visit Willem. Back in Baton Rouge I wait two weeks, and then give my friend the Dutchman a call and tell him that I cannot accept the Brazil offer, as it being unrealistic. He is suddenly not my friend anymore and when I put down the phone I have to laugh. Much to my surprise, I get a call from the director a few days later. He agrees that the Brazilian offer is not realistic but then he enquires if I would accept a position with them in Canada. This is a tempting offer, however in the meantime I have received confirmation from the FAO that Syria has approved my appointment and they offer me a contract with the organization. I mention this development to the director, who comments 'so you choose the other side'. Still we depart on a cordial note. When I recall the story to Dr. Newsom, he laughs. 'This director knew he had to do something to protect the image of his company' he says 'Anyway I am happy to learn that you are going to Syria for the FAO'.

And then my time in America comes to an end.. I am expected to report at the FAO headquarters in Rome for my assignment in Syria. There are the goodbyes to friends, professors and fellow students. Shall we meet again!? And then I am on my flight from Baton Rouge to Rome. A new experience in my life has begun.

LSU, professor and students

LSU students in the field

Cotton, IPM and the FAO

The opportunity to work for the Food and Agricultural Organization of the United Nations (FAO) is a very special one. I feel really privileged when I get an offer to work for the organization as an IPM specialist on cotton in Syria. For years on end I have carried out research on IPM on cotton and soybeans in America. Finally I can apply my expertise on an international scale and that is a tremendous challenge. In order to understand my excitement it is necessary to explain in some detail the relationship between the concepts; cotton, IPM and the FAO.

Cotton

What a beautiful and useful crop and how nice it is slogging through recently irrigated cotton fields. Vastness, sheer blue sky, blazing sun, the midday air vibrating over the field at about 30 degrees Celsius. To be able to do original research here, the excitement of a new discovery, I am in hog heaven. A sentimental song? Yes, you can call it that, because a long lived dream is coming true.

The cotton plant belongs to the genus <u>Gossypium</u>, the family Bombacaceae, order Malvales. It is an important industrial crop, which is cultivated worldwide on about 30 million hectares. The main producers are China, the United States and India. Cotton is originally a perennial plant, which is cultivated as an annual crop for optimal harvest results. The plant needs much sun and water and is therefore grown best in a tropical or subtropical climate. Depending on variety and climate the growth period lasts about 150-215 days.

Seed germination takes about five days and needs a ground temperature of 15 -30 degrees Celsius. After about 45 days the first squares are formed, followed by the emergence of flowers and ovaries (pin bolls) at around 60 – 70 days. It takes about 40 – 60 days for the fruits (bolls) to open and then after about 60 days the lint can be harvested.

Many insects are feeding on cotton and the plant is also susceptible to fungi and bacteria. The use of pesticides on cotton is extensive. This practice has caused severe problems in many areas and in some cases cotton cultivation was not profitable any more.

Integrated Pest Management (IPM)

IPM uses a variety of control methods to keep a harmful insect population below levels that may cause major economic harm. This part of agricultural research, namely the protection of an agricultural crop against insect pests is both an extensive and fascinating science. In 2007 the animal kingdom counted some 1.250 million species of which 950 thousand were insects. Therefore, the importance of insects cannot be emphasized enough.

An IPM program can consist of the following components:

1. Cultural methods; - ground cultivation during a certain period – time of planting – crop rotation.
2. Biological control – ensuring population volumes of predators an parasites.
3. Economic threshold levels – pest population levels, which can be tolerated without causing economic yields losses.
4. Control measures using fungi, viruses and bacteria.
5. Use of selective insecticides.
6. Use of resistant varieties.

The application of this method to control harmful insect populations resulted from a growing awareness that the sole reliance on insecticides had serious consequences. For example; outbreaks of secondary pest species, the destruction of beneficial insect populations and the associated charges for cultivating an agricultural crop.

The use of insecticides started around 1860 against massive infestations of the Colorado beetle on potatoes. The insecticidal characteristic of DDT, as being a very effective organic insecticide, was detected in 1940. Over the next 25 years the use of insecticides increased dramatically, they were highly effective in controlling harmful insects in agricultural crops and also contributed to the medical health of both man and animal. Thousands of organic chemicals have been developed since, making for a very powerful industry.

Controlling insect pests with insecticides resulted in many significant successes. It appeared however that their widespread use resulted in insect populations, which grew resistant to insecticides, while non-target organisms were killed as well.

Because predators and parasites recover less quickly than plant feeding insects, some of these species which were before not harmful were now in a position to develop in a more serious pest than the harmful species of the past.

Under the auspices of the FAO, a panel of experts took the initiative to promote the IPM concept worldwide. A global FAO program on IPM started in 1978. I was one of the experts privileged to work in relevant cotton programs in the Middle East, Pakistan and Sudan.

To develop an effective IPM program for a certain crop, much research has to be carried out. An intimate knowledge, of the various insect pests and their feeding habits during the different growth stages of the plant, is needed. Also, very important, are the economic harvest losses procured per different infestation levels of pest insects.

The United Nations Food and Agriculture Organization (FAO)

FAO has its headquarters in Rome. The organization has the task to coordinate international efforts to fight hunger worldwide. FAO is also actively involved in to reduce rural poverty, including the development of rural employment, social protection and to help countries to prepare against natural and human-induced disasters, (*Wikipedia*).

I have sent an application to the FAO in Rome in July 1978. My professor gave me a heads up of IPM projects under development. He feels that I stand a good chance to work for the organization. I am eligible for a position in Syria but it takes several months before the appointment is a reality. It was waiting for the approval of the Syrian government.

At the end of November I fly from Baton Rouge Louisiana to Rome. I enter for the first time that imposing building of the FAO at the Via delle Terme di Caracalla and meet with the head of the department for *Agriculture Plant Protection Service* (AGPP). Dr. Lucas Brader, a Dutchman, is a dynamic man, and reputed for his work on plant protection in the tropics. He takes me under his wing and introduces me to colleagues and the department's administrative staff. I'm also presented to the big boss of the *Agriculture Plant Production and Protection Division* (AGP), under which comes the AGPP department. We have a good talk and he puts me at ease. I feel embraced by a global family and that is a very special feeling after having lived for years as a sort of monk. He tells me that his daughter and son-in-law are working in Syria and that it is a beautiful country, where I shall feel at home in no time.

There's one thing I haven't realized yet: This is a tremendous opportunity to conduct original work; to research an insect fauna that is largely unknown. As I haven't seen my family for the past two years, I ask for a ten days leave before going to Syria. My request is granted, and Mid-December I shall leave the Netherlands for Damascus to start my work in Syria. These days with my mother in her flat, the visits with brothers and sister are important. The years I spent in America were very special and tough. Now I need to adjust to a more normal daily rhythm, to rekindle the bond with family and friends again.

Syria, a world appointment
(1978 – 1983)

The beginning

When I arrive in Damascus, December 1970, I am met by a broad smiling man, who introduces himself as Abdul Azim H. He speaks good German, because he worked for many years in Germany, he tells me. He is now in charge of the fleet of cars of the national Cotton Bureau in Aleppo, the FAO associate partner for this project. Damascuas is my first acquaintance with the Arabic world. I don't sleep much that night, because there are many new impressions to deal with.

The next day at 2.00 o'clock in the afternoon Abdul collects me in the project car, a Peugeot 504 station, which he cleared through customs a few days ago. We are off to Aleppo, first through the chaotic traffic of Damascus, but once out of town it is more quiet and we can talk. Dr Hussein sends his regards. He is the project manager and my direct superior and he expects me at the office as soon as possible.

That evening we stop somewhere at a restaurant Abdul knows very well. I have my first Arabic meal, which I really enjoy. Abdul urges me to also drink a glass of Tiger milk, a kind of anisette or Pernod drink, but then somewhat stronger. Abdul knows many people here. The local police chief sits down at our table and the evening is really getting enjoyable. Late that night we arrive in Aleppo. A room has been booked for me at the Ramsis hotel in the main street. Until I have found a permanent residence, this will be my home for the next few weeks. Abdul asks me at what time to morrow I like to come to the office . " Would 8.30 o'clock be possible"? I ask tentatively? "But of course, fine and Abdul shall collect me. It was a pleasure *Herr Doctor"*

Day to day affairs

I meet with Dr. Hussein E., a short heavyset man of Palestinian descent but now a national of Jordan. There is small talk, on Rome, the travel and family. Hussein introduces me to the directors of the Cotton Bureau and to Mr. Mushid E., a deputy director, who is the national coordinator of the project and who works directly with Dr. Hussein. I also meet the agricultural engineers, Hassan I. and Majid N., who will work directly with me. I also get to know George, an old employee of the Cotton Bureau, with whom I shall share an office.

And then a tall Englishman enters the office, who introduces himself as Tony M. He is a FAO expert in a sister project on agricultural mechanization. Tony is here the mechanic and calls himself a *"hand and spanner"* man. He arrived three months earlier in Syria and is glad to see a Western face, although it is not an English mug. There is direct contact and after office time,at 2.00 o'clock in the afternoon we take lunch in the Baron hotel, directly opposite my hotel. Tony served nine years as a paratrooper in the British army. He is married and has a son, but the family lives in England. Soon we are every afternoon after work together. I help him to paint his flat's interior for the upcoming visit of his wife and child.

He shows me around Aleppo, and we look for living quarters for me.

Through Tony I get to know the daughter of the AGP director and her husband. Egbert K. and his wife Alicia have two small children and live in the town Rakka, about two hours drive from Aleppo. Egbert works in a large German development project, which has the objective to construct an Institute for Agricultural Mechanization and to train also local instructors. The project is financed by the German Development Organization of the Ministry of Foreign Affairs (GTZ). It includes three more German experts, who all live with their families in Rakka. There is soon regular contact with visits here and there and especially Egbert becomes a good friend. When he has to be in Aleppo he stays with me and when there is a party in Rakka I stay with him and his family.

Early January '79, I find with the help of a kind of a real-estate agent a suitable and affordable flat. It is a furnished ground floor apartment, with a living room a small sunroom, a kitchen, bathroom and bedroom. It's basically a lean-to of the homeowner's residence, a well to-do Syrian, who is quite pleased to rent this flat to me. The apartment is equipped with two primitive oil stoves for heating and you have to learn how to operate these. You slightly open the oil supply for some diesel oil to enter the stove. Not too much mind you, otherwise there will be a boom when the stove is lighted. Once the oil is burning then you regulate the oil supply and air flow until there is a nice blue flame. You really cannot leave the stoves unattended. It is January, the weather is cold and drizzly. Without heating the flat is really cold. That first week in my new accommodation I leave for work in the morning and keep the stoves burning. Upon my return in the afternoon, the landlord is waiting for me. Through the window he has seen his stoves burning and he knows they are very unreliable. With tears in his eyes he begs me not to keep the stoves burning when I'm not at home, because of fire hazard. Indeed a few times the stoves go out, while the oil keeps on flowing., so that suddenly I have a stove full of diesel oil, which, just in time, I do not ignite.

Wheels

Hussein has a project car, a Peugeot 504 station with air conditioning. Also for me a project car is being ordered. Hussein assumes that I also want to have air- conditioning in the car but then he is mistaken. When working in the field in temperatures over the 30 degrees Celsius, the transition from a cold interior to a hot dusty field is not healthy. There is then also the temptation to take it easy and to stay in the cool interior. This might result in a slowdown in the tempo of work. This wisdom I learned in the hot cotton and soybean fields of Louisiana. The professor was not in favor of air con-ditioned pick-up trucks. His comment: 'You young people and especially you Stam do not need this'. At first Hussein does not understand my reasoning and Mushid, as an office man, even less so, but I succeed to convince them. It will take however four months before the car can be delivered in Syria, which means that I can start far too late with my fieldwork. Therefore I need to find my own car as quickly as possible. Together with Tony I visit several secondhand car dealers in Aleppo but they don't have much to offer and then at exorbitant high prices. I am more successful in Damascus. As a FAO staff member I have diplomatic status and I'm thus allowed to either buy in the Free Trade Zone or else to import a car duty-free. However this duty-free privilege is only valid for the first six months of residence. I decide to try my luck in the Free Trade Zone, as the quickest way to obtain wheels, since time is getting short. I am in luck; there are two cars for sale; an Opel Record and a Fiat. I choose the Opel, we settle on the price and then with a handshake the deal is closed. I make a down payment and I get two weeks to pay the balance as otherwise the deal is off.

I can obtain a loan from the FAO, which I have to repay each month through deductions on my salary. Within ten days I am back in the Free Zone and the Opel is mine and yes against a sharp prize. The dealer tells me smiling that he already has had two higher bids than what I had to pay for it. The UN is however an important client and yes, he loves me. Well that is of course touching, but the transport manager of the UN, who has assisted me in every way, knows how business is done in the second hand car business in Damascus.

That I have made a good buy is confirmed. From the Free Zone I drive directly to a garage for an inspection and to make sure there is oil in the gearbox and cardan house. With secondhand cars and certainly in the Far East you cannot accept anything at face value. 'Well what is this car worth' I ask the mechanic. He looks appreciative, names a price, which makes me very happy.

That evening my pride stands glittering in front of the hotel. Together with Hussein and Mushid I drove to Damascus, where they participated in a meeting at the Ministry of Agriculture. I am congratulated on both my new purchase and the fact that I passed my Syrian driving license test. My Dutch permit was namely not acknowledged as sufficient proof of my ability to drive a car. The following day Mushid drives with me back to Aleppo.

Work

Together with Hussein I visit the faculty of Plant Protection of the University of Aleppo. We meet the head of the department, Dr. G. Hariri, whom I like straight away. We drink the customary glass very sweet thee and we talk. Dr. Hariri is of the opinion that the FAO project should collaborate with his department and not the Cotton Bureau. And what is my opinion. I don't commit myself and let Dr. Hussein do the talking. I completely agree with him that the Cotton Bureau is the right national institute to work with our project.

The following Sunday, Hariri collects me at 9.00 o'clock in the morning to show me his field laboratory. Near the village Mushlemieh, North of Aleppo, he has a modest little cottage, with three rooms, in which a few tables and chairs, some glassware and a few damaged insect cages. There is also a field of 1000 m2 with stalks of old cotton plants. Hariri makes thee, lights his pipe, settles himself in the one and only easy chair, and tells me that I should be able to work here very pleasantly. I make an effort to explain to him that I intend to work directly in farmer's fields, because we need data about what is happening out there.

On our way back we visit the local brewery. The director is a good friend of Hariri and he feels that I should really taste this beer. Hariri is getting to be a friend over the next four years. He meets with much opposition but puts life in perspective and remains in the best of spirits.

The work program

Cultivation of cotton in Syria; about 138810 ha were planted in 1980 of which 57 % along the river's the Euphrates and Khabur, 19% on the Aleppo plain, 22% around the cities Hamma and Homs and 2% in the neighborhood of Damascus. It is not known when cotton was first cultivated in Syria. Untill 1927 there were yearly no more than 800 ha, but the area had increased till 30491 ha in 1937. After the 2nd world war the area increased significantly to 217000 ha in 1951, while 302000 ha were harvested in 1962. Cotton in Syria is planted from mid April till mid May. The harvest takes place between the end of September till mid November.

In order to get a better idea about my experiences in Syria, a description of my work is necessary. My task is manifold and also very interesting, because there is little known about the cotton fauna in Syria. I can therefore do pioneering work in my professional field and that is a privilege and very special.

In first instance it has to be investigated, which are the beneficial and harmful insects occurring in cotton. Then there is the matter of yield loss due to the various insect pest species. We also have to find out to what extend beneficial insects inhibit feeding by phytophagous insects and associated yield loss. With this information in hand a strategy can be developed to control harmful insect populations in an ecological safe manner; the concept IPM.

Throughout 1979 I have been able to gather much information on the various growth stages of cotton and the insect populations present at the time in three regions of Syria; around Aleppo, along the Euphrates near Rakka and in the Deir ez Zor area. That same year insect populations were surveyed in other crops as well, i.e. alfalfa, maize, wheat, sugar beets, potatoes and beans.

The main cotton insect pest appears to be the spiny bollworm (*Earias insulana*), which especially in the Deir ez Zor area causes much damage. A second important pest in that area is the shedder bug (*Creotiades pallidus*), which causes the so called "shamragha" (tall growing plants with an excessive shedding of fruiting forms) (3). The European boll worm (*Heliothis armigera*) can cause damage too.

During the next three years I study the relationship between the insect pests; European and spiny boll worms and the insect predators; coccinellids, predator mirids (*Reduvidae*

Anthocoridae), tall mirids (*Lygaeidae*), chrysopids and spiders. We also discover that bollworm eggs are being parasitized by minute wasps (*Trichogrammatidae*) and that the worms themselves are a source of food for yet another wasp (*Braconidae*). Furthermore we learn that the nymphal instars of the white fly (*Bemisia tabaci*) are attacked by tiny wasps (*Aphelinidae*).(4)

It appears that all those predators and parasites play an important role in controlling populations of bollworms and whiteflies. It also becomes very clear that insecticides, when used at the wrong time, disturb the balance in a cotton agro ecosystem by decimating the beneficial insects.

Field work

One of my tasks is therefore to identify the beneficial insects living in cotton in Syria. There are a few commonly known insect pests for which insecticides are being used, but further no reliable information is available. The most important objective of our project is therefore avoiding the unnecessary use of insecticides, by introducing the concept IPM.

I discuss with Hussein what has to be done and prepare a plan of work. In three regions where cotton is cultivated I want to monitor four elements; the development of the cotton plant, the presence of useful and harmful insects, damage inflicted to leaves, fruiting forms and the subsequent harvest results.

We select three fields; one near the village Muslimieh, North of Aleppo, one near the town of Rakka, about two hours drive East of Aleppo and one around the town of Deir ez Zor, located in the East of Syria along the Euphrates. As soon as the cotton seed has germinated and the first leaves are above ground, I start with my weekly field visits in these three areas. In Aleppo, the two agricultural engineers of the

Cotton Bureau are pleasant and conscientious co-workers. Every Monday morning, starting in April, we drive together to our field in Muslimieh. Our various observations keep us busy until the afternoon. Flying insects are caught with an insect sweepnet and stored in plastic bags, to be later counted in the laboratory. It is exhausting work, especially during the summer months with temperatures over 30 degrees C. After about six hours we are finished. Bathed in sweat we get into the car and drive back to the office, tired but satisfied after a job well done.

Then, on Tuesday morning I drive to Rakka, where I meet around 10.00 o'clock my fellow worker of the Plant Protection Service. Together with Lutli M., I go to our field where we make our observations until mid afternoon. Cotton fields in Syria are flooded regularlys, because the plants need much water. Often we stand ankle deep in the mud, a source of some hilarious moments. Often a young agricultural engineer, an assistant of Lutli accompanies us to assist with the observations. Lutli considers it to be a form of training for the young fellows. It is something to get used to for the young man, proud of his title and the respective social standing in his community. Traipsing around the mud barefooted, going down on your knees between endless rows of cotton plants, counting fruiting forms, worms and other insects! It is something to get used to.

It is humid and hot in that field, generally well over 35 degrees C. He has no choice, because his boss sits also in the mud and that Dutchman seems to be swimming in it. And then he tries to stand up, but is unable to move, with both legs firmly stuck in the mud. He sways to and fro, like a tree in a storm wind and then tips over. Covered in mud he can laugh with us, an experience richer.

Then the work is finished. It is 4.00 o'clock in the afternoon and we go over to Lutli his house. We wash and I put on a pair of clean trousers. It feels good to relax after working in those hot fields. The heath has made us languid and a little snooze would now be very welcome, but I have to go on. Lutli's wife has prepared a meal and we eat in friendly fellowship. Lutli is a faithful Muslim. There is a dialogue with mutual respect for each other's profession of faith. Then I am on my way to Deir-ez-Zor, another drive of two hours. Wednesday I make here my observations. In Deir-ez-Zor there is a sister FAO project located, which has a guest house for its staff members, when they are visiting the project. Other UN personnel can also make use of this accommodation.

That first year, Deir ez Zor's local administration is not very cooperative. The chef of the Plant Protection Service, Adnan Kh., has studied a few years in Egypt and is not exactly trilled to meet me. He accompanies me once into the field, but then he has seen enough. To squat between plants in the mud for a few hours is not for him; for that work he has his assistants. And no, he has no engineers available to work with me, so sorry. So I have no choice but to make all the observations by myself and that means overtime.

Then Thursday morning I drive directly from Deir-ez-Zor to Aleppo. That afternoon and Friday are used to count and identify the insects collected in the several fields that past week. There are many samples to go through and soon there is a growing backlog, so that many samples are stored in the freezer.

In the cotton fields near Deir-ez-Zor, where I make every week my observations, the plants grow very tall and shed many flower buds and little bolls. (fruiting forms). This results in very few full grown bolls and a severe reduction in yield. My Sudanese colleague, Dr. Abdul L., the agronomist in the sister FAO project, has observed this phenomenon earlier and in his opinion it is caused by an insect. I agree with him and I soon think that I may have found the culprit. During my observations I count large numbers of a plant bug (*mirids*) and by doing several specific experiments and making detailed observations, I am able to conclude that the shedder bug (*Creontiades pallidus*), is the reason for this excessive shedding, which locally is called "*shamragha*". Hussein is happy, because this means that our project has detected a new insect pest for cotton in Syria.

And so the season 1979 passes by. Between April and November I make my weekly rounds of Aleppo, Rakka, and Deir-ez-Zor and feel entirely at home. The hours of fieldwork, the panoramic views, the interaction with local co-workers and inhabitants; they are all aspects of my work, which makes it so interesting. Then there are the winter months, but there is enough work to be done. Reports have to be written, we give lectures and trainings, and the many collected insects have to be counted and identified. Also field work continues, because where do all these harmful and beneficial insects remain between the months of November and April, when there is no crop in the field? The winter months are also the period to take our holidays, because during the season there is no time for that.

Engagement

December 1979: I will spend a couple of weeks in the Netherlands. I have corresponded with a young lady, whom I have met through friends in America and we became pen pals. Now we are going to meet for the first time during this holiday season.

All in all it becomes a memorable month. When I arrive at Schiphol airport I take possession of my rental car and ten minutes later I am on my way to Gorssel, where mother lives in a retirement home. So I miss the whole family, who are waiting for me in the arrival hall, an initiative of mother. That week I get engaged. Annemiek, the object of my devotion, is fifteen years my junior and starry eyed in love. She believes; they lived long and happily. I am forty, naïve in love and believe with her. When I tell mother the happy news, she is so relieved she has to sit down. She really worried about this unmarried son, always on the go to faraway lands.

The first time I meet the family of Annemiek is in the village of Diever, where her parents have a holiday home. They are all very curious about this unbelievable He-man Annemiek has snared. On Saturday morning I drive to the holiday home, where I am received as the prodigal son. I am placed in a chair, facing her father, mother, brothers and sister sitting in a half circle opposite me and then I am subjected to a cross examination. Annemiek sits next to me, holds my hand in a firm grip and makes that I behave myself. One night we take her parents to a fancy restaurant inLeiden and that is for me, man of innocence, an experience. Little pieces of meat are presented with much endeavor. Of course we keep telling that this dish is something very special in taste and preparation. The wine performance is really something special and of course you don't look for the price! After the dessert a kind of "watch out don't choke", I am still kind of hungry, but that is good for the figure and yes for that insight you pay. The steep bill and tip give me indigestion but the ladies are presented with red roses, which are fitted on their coats with much élan. We are appreciated, valued friends of the business. Please realize, not just everyone is honored with a pretty little rose like that.

Turmoil in the country

January 1980: I am back in Aleppo. It is cold and drizzly

weather and dust has changed into mud, so it is impossible to keep shoes and trousers tidy. My car has a damaged battery, the stoves in the apartment are difficult to get burning and Hussein has not returned from Jordan yet. All in all my homecoming leaves much to be desired. Perhaps it is due to the miserable weather, but there is a kind of depressive mood in the town.

For me there is a bright spot though; Annemiek, my new fiancée, will visit me in April. The prices of food in the restaurant, where I daily have ny dinner each afternoon after work, are rapidly increasing. This is getting ridiculous and I decide it is time to start cooking myself. Some time ago I received from my sister Maartje a cookbook. She thought it was high time that I learned to take care of myself, and as a loving sister she decided to support me hereby. That little book proves now to be very useful. I study receipts, buy pots and pans and other kitchen utensils and get on with it. I buy potatoes, tinned vegetables, meats, fruits and other comestibles and start preparing my first meals. I must admit, it is fun, gives satisfaction and makes for more diversity in my domestic activities.

Many times I my life I had the feeling that a guardian angel was watching over me. Early March there is suddenly a general strike. Shops are closed and also restaurants do not serve food anymore. The army enters the city and a curfew is imposed. One evening I go out for my usual run. Suddenly there is a lot of shouting and I am summoned to a halt. Two fellows, dressed in a kind of uniform are advancing on me with cocked Kalashnikov rifles, which they trust into my stomach. The men are very tense, suspicious and are shouting at me. I try to make them feel at ease, put up my hands and relax. 'Hé, take it easy, oké nothing wrong, I live around here and I am now going home, good evening'. It is clear, the safety situation in Aleppo has detoriated.

One sunny morning I get into my car and drive as usual to the office. The streets are deserted and the people I see are standing around aimlessly. Near the Cotton Bureau a tank is stationed. The street is barricaded and with hand gestures I am instructed by the soldiers to go away. I try to reach the office by another route but with the same result. I have no other option then to return to my apartment. I feel very fortunate that I bought food and decided to cook for myself.

During the past year I have gotten to know several people of ICARDA (*International Center for Agricultural Research in the dry Areas*). One morning Jean, a young Belgian scientist and two female colleagues, pay me a visit. They have concluded that it has become too dangerous in Aleppo and a group of ICARDA personnel has decided to depart that morning for Damascus and to await further developments there. I am invited to join them. It seems that the Muslim Brotherhood intends to dispose of the government of president Assad. I tell Jean that I do not believe that we are in danger in Aleppo and that it is not the right thing to do, leaving everything at the first signs of unrest. 'No old chap, I don't see any reason to drive all the way to Damascus, I am pretty busy' I tell him.

My advice is ignored. They feel that the situation is getting worse and they have warned me!! Not everyone in ICARDA has panicked. The program manager, who lives close by, pays me also a visit. We agree that we have to stay calm and that we should keep each other informed on future developments.

However, I take into account that I cannot visit Deir ez Zor for a while, to make preparations for my research program the coming season. In one of my experiments I want to plant plots with alfalfa between cotton fields This experiment has to be sown in early April. Through a radio message I request the UNDP(*United Nations Development Program*) office to send a message to the FAO Agricultural project in Deir ez Zor with the request to prepare fields with cotton interspersed with alfalfa fields.

Aleppo has now also become to the attention of the Diplomatic Service of the Netherlands in Damascus. One morning there is a radio message for me from the UNDP office. It is a request from the Embassy of the Netherlands; if I can meet with two representatives of the Embassy for lunch at the Baron hotel at such and such a date.

When we get together there is first some small talk and then there is a request. There is much going on in the country. Aleppo is regularly in the news and the Embassy would like to know what is going on. And if I would mind to be their man in Aleppo so to speak, ha,ha,ha, They watch me expectantly, since this is a very special request. To be asked by the Dutch Government to act as a sort of spy, That is a honor!!? For a moment I don't know what to say, overcome by this unexpected interest in little old me. But then I can think clearly again and tell the man that as a FAO expert I have no time for this Endeavour, I have other responsibilities. They are clearly disappointed, and I actually have to laugh a little because I rather like the two men. So I continue, saying that when I hear and see something that could be important I shall inform them when I happen to be in Damascus and yes I expect then a nice meal in return.

Day to Day Affairs

In March 1980 the security situation has gone back to normal and it is again possible to travel upcountry. The cur view has been lifted and shops and restaurants are open again for business. I am relieved because a continued security problem would have seriously hampered our program.

I have planned an extensive research program, mainly in the Deir ez Zor region, because here are the most severe insect problems in cotton. This means that during the season I shall stay in Deir ez Zor four days a week. So I have to find living quarters there because we plan that Annemiek is going to stay with me for two months during the summer. We have to find out if we can live in harmony together. Especially for Annemiek everything will be new and very strange.

My national coworker for the Deir ez Zor region knows a certain house owner, who has his first floor apartment for hire. It is May, the flat looks fine and I am happy. Two furnished rooms, a small balcony, this will be fun. Annemiek arrives on the 4th of June. We spend a few nice days in Aleppo and then we move to Deir ez Zor. The apartment is not a success. It is really very hot inside. In the field it is already over the 30 degrees Celcius. With the sun directly above the flat roof it is in the flat in the afternoon soon over 40 degrees, an oven. It is not possible to sleep by this heath. At night I lay stretched out on the terrazzo floor, for me the only way to catch some sleep. Annemiek tries to cool down with the help of wet towels. I need to find a different accommodation and we are in luck. Near Deir ez Zor there is a beet sugar mill with an adjacent camp for its personnel. It consists of a few prefabricated bungalows and several barracks with single bedrooms, all of them equipped with air conditioning. In the summer months the mill is not in operation and the majority of the labor force has gone back home. I get to know the manager, an Austrian, who lives with his family in one of the bungalows. Adolf is an amiable family man and he is in charge of the maintenance crew, which has to prepare the mill for the upcoming sugar beet campaign.

We can rent one of the bungalows for the summer months and that is really good news. Adolf is also happy since he has a young couple as his neighbor and that will be also nice for his family. A few more families live in the camp, Italians and Tjechoslovakians, and soon we get to know everybody and is there social contact. The bungalows are furnished and consist of a living room, bedroom, bathroom and a little kitchen. After having been in the hot fields the whole day, coming home is now a real pleasure, the house a place of repose and coolness.

The work routine remains the same. We are in Deir ez Zor four days and then on Thursday afternoon, after field work is done we drive to Aleppo. On Friday I make the observations in the Aleppo area and then on Monday we go back to Deir ez Zor. For Annemiek this is a way of life to get used to. It is not easy for her to adjust to a hot desert environment after a sheltered life in Leiden the Netherlands. Sure, she is with her fiancé now but that man is very busy with his work those months and is the whole day on the go.

However, we have a nice time. Key for me is, I am not alone anymore. In the evening when I come home from work, Annemiek has prepared a nice meal. We relax in the nice coolness of the house and we talk and get to know each other better. It is for the first time since our engagement last December that we are together again. Her father advised her 'Annemiek, now don't be in a hurry but find out if you can live with this man, if you can identify with his way of life, so much different than living in the Netherlands'. At times she is uncertain and afraid for the unknown, especially when the man does not want to talk, just too tired from a busy day in the field. But then they talk and her mind is put at ease again. One thing she learns. His work, his research in those hot cotton fields is very important to him and almost everything else comes second.

Notwithstanding the intensive work schedule we also sometimes go out for some socializing. One afternoon, after work, we visit Deir ez Zor town, together with Adolf, his wife Mertle and their two daughters. In the local ice parlor we enjoy a nice sorbet. The two Western women and especially Annemiek are ogled minutely by many gleaming dark eyes. In this tiny dessert town, blond hair and blue eyes are something very special. One young fellow is so bewitched by Annemiek that a scoop of ice ends up in his ear, instead of his mouth to the great amusement of everybody present. In the local market I sometimes have to grumble to keep pushy men at bay.

Annemiek flies back to Holland early September to prepare for the wedding. I follow at the end of October and then in November the wedding takes place. A relationship which will not last long; there are just too many differences in our perception of life and our priorities.

Work

My relationship with Hussein is not exactly easy those first two years. He is of the old school, an authoritarian, and he has difficulty to understand what I am trying to do. Despite that I respect and like him. He is honest, very direct and treats everyone the same, indiscriminate of their social standing, when something is not correct according to his standard and it is an attitude that does not make him friends. He does understand however that we first have to start out with more general initial investigations to find out the actual problems in terms of insects and of cotton growing in Syria. However he prefers to cultivate many beneficial insects and to release them in the fields. This method is straightforward, easy to understand and to explain to the Ministry of Agriculture,

Department Plant Protection and the management of the Cotton Bureau.

It takes some effort to convince him of my way of thinking; to make use of the local existing population of beneficial insects in cotton. We have to try to reduce the use of insecticides by means of establishing Economic Injury levels for the different insect pest species. When we can achieve this, by carrying out experiments, then we have lasting results, which can save the Syrian government a lot of money. Slowly but surely Hussein gets more confidence in my philosophy of work and our professional relationship improves.

Hussein keeps on going. One of his tasks is to introduce the FAO IPM regional project also in the other countries in the region. He visits Irak a few times and he has also talks with the Ministry of Agriculture in Turkey. Here the authorities would really like to start a project in the Cukorova region, the lowlands along the South coast, around the town Adana. In this area much cotton is cultivated and insecticides are used on a large scale, which has caused a gigantic problem with the insect pest the white fly (*Bemisia tabaci*). When this project will come through I shall be transferred to Turkey to get the program organized. All kinds of interesting developments.

Consultants

Oscar B.,our first consultant, works with us for three weeks in August 1980. He is from Peru and an autodidact, who has much experience with biological control in cotton. After an "feeling out", we work well together and I learn new methods of observation, which prove to be very useful. It is a pleasure to be out in the fields with him and to learn to recognize several interactions between different insect species.

Early August 1981, two eminent members of my field of study are visiting. The American Thomas L. is a distinguished professor at the University of California. He is an authority on plant bugs and the damage they cause to the cotton plant. He is a large, very friendly man, who lets me indirectly know that he likes what I am trying to accomplish in Syria. He knows everything of the plant bug,*Creontiades pallidus* and the shamragha problem and his advice is important for my research.

Henry F.,his colleague consultant, is an Englishman and an old colonial cotton veteran, who really knows the plant and who has worked for years in the Sudan. In the beginning he is somewhat reserved towards me, but when he notes that I listen to him and want to learn, he becomes very cooperative and lets me share in his extensive knowledge of the cotton plant.

Hussein enters into an agreement with the ODA (Overseas Development Administration), England in 1981, to carry out a Pheromone project for the spiny bollworm. Pheromones are chemical lures, that attract the moths. The objective is to reduce the populations by installing many Pheromone traps in the cotton fields. Derek C. is in charge of this project. After a first "wait and see" period he gets into his own and I keep laughing about his dry English humor. It is always a pleasure to exchange experiences after work under the enjoyment of an alcoholic refreshment.

Family life

Our last year in Syria, 1982, is a good and productive period. We are now a little family. Thomas, our son is born in Leiden, November 1981 and I can take part in this major happening in our life. Annemiek is very sociable and makes easily contact with people. Soon we have a busy social life with dinner engagements and parties here and there and by us at home. Most of our acquaintances work with ICARDA and live in our neighborhood. This give a lot of sociability, especially for Annemiek and her circle of women friends. Before we married I was able to rent a large ground floor apartment and yes with central heating. We have now a large living room, two bed rooms, bathroom and kitchen.

It has always been a long time wish of mother to visit this son of hers, who always works abroad. Until now it never happened. Once there were plans to visit America, but the health of father was not good and therefore he did not have the spirit of enterprise for this Endeavour. Mother is now a widow, very clear headed, in good health and now it has to happen. Riet, her daughter in law, loves to come along. It will be for here a maiden flight, because she has never been in a plane before. Brother Klaas will not come along. He does not like flying and besides he has to work.

It becomes a very special visit, with for me some very tense moments. They arrive at Damascus airport in the evening of 5 December 1982. I have booked rooms in a hotel and the ladies go to bed very soon after the long and exhausting journey. The plan is to start early next morning for the five hours drive to Aleppo. I get a nasty surprise when I look out of my window at 7.00 o'clock the next morning. There is a leaden sky and it is snowing and that is very unusual for Syria. It becomes a rigorous journey in foul weather with mother and Riet in the back and I stretched to the limit behind the wheel. The traffic in Damascus is as usual a wild Endeavour and the snow and mud make the going especially hazardous. After one hour of tacking, shifting gears, braking and giving gas, we are out of the city and we start to climb. It is now snowing heavily and it is getting colder. Mother and Riet are huddled together in the back with a blanket over their legs. My Opel Record is a very good car but not exactly equipped for winter circumstances. The heather does not work and there is no antifreeze in the window washers. We drive now through a white world with hardly any traffic on the road, which is marked by telephone poles and car tracks. This circumstance is very unexpected and the last thing which I have anticipated. I am worried about mother, When we get stuck here we have a serious problem. Every so often I have to stop to clear the wind shield from ice . On one occasion I get into a slide, but with an instinctive steering movement and giving controlled gas I manage to get the car on the road again. I am really focused to the utmost with only one thought, we are going to reach Aleppo. We drive on through a white world. The women in the back are doing fine and keep quiet, very much aware of the very unusual situation. I have noticed this with mother before. In difficult situations she is always very relaxed and not easily perturbed. She is mentally a very strong woman. Riet is a "trooper", who always likes a new experience.

After a journey of ten hours we arrive in snow covered Aleppo, where Annemiek and Thomas welcome oma and aunt Riet. I have no holiday and work needs to be done. Hussein and myself visit the Institute of Plant Protection of the Ministry of Agriculture of Turkey in Adana, from 12 till 16 December, to discuss the forthcoming program in Turkey for the coming year. When we are back in Aleppo it is beautiful weather. In the weekend we make trips in the surroundings and my women enjoy that particular world which is Syria, so very different of Holland.

There is a party by friends and the four of us go there. The daughter of friends likes to take care of Thomas and she knows where the party is taking place. Riet is the star of the evening. And I hardly recognize her. She talks with everybody in a kind of pidgin English and performs a solo dance show, which is admired by everyone. Mother does not dance but she enjoys herself tremendously. The young people of the different nationalities around her admire and respect her mental vitality. And then the visit is coming to an end. One sunny, beautiful day we drive to Damascus, a journey so much different than the winter trip a fortnight ago.

Women, who live in a small community in a foreign culture, not able to work outdoors and therefore restricted to each other's company. Their men engaged in interesting and challenging work, which takes much energy and time. It can easily cause problems in relationships in a community. An old grumpy professor at the Tropical College in Deventer, with many years of working in the tropics, had warned us young students one time about this occurrence. 'Dam, the trouble always started with the women'.

Suddenly, there is a problem. Nutsi, the wife of Willem, is angry with Annemiek, who can be very hoity toity, when she gets angry. It is impossible to get to her. The pleasant "get togethers" with Willem, the husband of Nutsi and a soil scientist with ICARDA and a few other Dutchmen are over. I drink with Willem one evening a few beers and we curse this business between our women. It means that we cannot see each other anymore, if we value to stay married. Annemiek is happy when we hear in September that the project in Turkey is going through and that we shall move to Adana early 1983.

The Last Strech

And then, at long last there is the confirmation that the project in Turkey is a go. The UNEP (UN Environmental Protection Agency) is going to finance the program for one year and we are optimistic that the program will then be extended through another donor. It is the start of very busy period. I have to finalize my program in Syria and write the 1982 end report. Organize transport for our personal belongings from Aleppo to Adana and then say goodbye to all our friends, and colleagues in Damascus, Aleppo, Rakka and Deir ez Zor. I have to export two cars from Syria to Turkey and that requires much paperwork and patience. We have to move quickly. By the end of March we need to be settled in Adana, because in April the cotton seed is planted in the Cukorova region and then our program there has to start.

My project car, the Peugeot station, is going with me to Turkey and that exercise I shall not easily forget. On the 28th February 1983 I drive the car to the Syrian border and I am cleared through customs without a problem. Through no man's land I drive to the Turkish border and here the problems start. The customs officer, a surly fellow, tells me that the car papers are not in order and that my nicely painted UN number plate is not valid in Turkey. He makes a casual gesture with his arm end tells me to return to Syria. Hé hallo, no way, the Syrians are not waiting for me. I talk a blue mile, show the man official letters and telephone with the FAO representative in Ankara, but the man is not willing to let me go. A Turkish driver on a Dutch truck is very helpful. He is able to convince the officer that I am working for the UN and that I have no money to convince him and that he better lets me pass, because otherwise there might be problems with his superior.

At long last, after a delay of five hours at the border I am allowed to drive on. I stay over in Iskanderun and the next day I drive by way of Adana to the FAO office in Ankara, which will register the car and obtain a valid UN number plate for Turkey. I fly back to Adana and from there I take the bus to Aleppo.

When boarding the bus at the bus station in Adana I am witness of a family scene., apparently people of a village in the neighborhood. The family consists of an eldery man and two women. One of the women is of the same age as the man and is completely ignored by the oddball fellow. The younger woman, with a little boy is clearly his favorite. His mumble mouth void of teeth is distorted in a grimace, which is supposed to be a laugh. He touches the hair of the little boy and you can see that his mother feels honored. Also in Syria I came across families of one man with several women..

When I am back in Aleppo there is another very busy month to finalize all outstanding business in Syria and then we are ready and eager to go. On 25 March 1983 we drive with our Opel car to the Syrian border. The entrance to Turkey occurs now without problems and once more stay over in Iskanderun, but now together with Annemiek and Thomas. When we arrive in Adana we check into a hotel. It is the start of out stay in Turkey.

An unconscious look in the far future

A particular incident which you hardly expected to be possible, but it occurred! When I arrived for the first time in Syria I visited the Embassy of the Netherlands in Damascus to register myself as a Dutch citizen, living in Syria. The entrance hall was adorned with a large poster "Promotion of the Netherlands". It showed a beautiful young woman in the traditional dress of Arnemuiden. In those days I was still a bachelor, dear reader, so please forgive my open salivating mouth. That poster really made a huge impression on me. Really impressive, Dutch glory. The truth really, on the 25th of May 1990, eleven years later, that very same beautiful young woman in the poster became my wife.

Turkey, memorable times (1983 – 1984)

March 1983: Our first accommodation is a hotel room in Adana. We have the address of a Dutch lady, who is married with a Turkish industrialist, friend of friends of the parents of Annemiek. We are getting in touch with Suzan A. and she is very helpful and hospitable. The last few months have been very tiring for me; my immune system lets me down and I have to stay in bed. Annemiek now takes over. Together with Suzan she goes searching for an apartment. After a few days she has found something and is really enthusiastic. I have recovered sufficiently to be able to accompany her and Suzan to look at the apartment. It is indeed very nice, well maintained with a large living room, three bedrooms, kitchen, toilet and bathroom and the rental price is very reasonable. We decide to rent it for one year and we are really happy.

Now we have to buy furniture, because we expect to live here for at least three years. In Adana there is not much choice so we have to go to Ankara for the necessary purchases. We fly with Thomas from Adana to Ankara. The paperwork to get the project car registered in Turkey has been completed by the FAO office and we can drive the car back from Ankara to Adana. We buy all the necessary furniture; tables, chairs, cupboards, curtains, a stove, fridge and three air conditioners. It is a lot of money which we spend, however "you have to lose a fly to catch a trout", and it is important that wife and child feel at home in a completely new environment.

About ten day later our purchases are delivered. In the meantime also our crate with personal belongings has arrived from Syria. Within a week our flat has become home, the air co's installed and working and we are settled. Now with the home front organized I can concentrate on my work. I am attached to the Regional Institute for Plant Protection and Research in Adana. The head of the cotton department is Achmed T. and he is my direct national coworker. He has a team of 10 fellow workers under whom several students, who gain here practical experience. Ahmed and myself soon work very well together. We both love to be out in the fields and to sit the whole day between cotton plants to make observations.

The work program

In Turkey, cotton is cultivated in eight regions. The Aegean with about 200.000 ha and the Mediterranean with about 400.000 ha are in 1986 the most important areas. The Mediterranean zone comprises five provinces of which Incel and Adana cover the Cekorova plain, the lowlands of Turkey. Here grows yearly about 265.000 ha cotton. During the 13 year period, 1970 – 1983, the average costs of crop protection were 24,3% of yield.

During this period three insect pests are responsible for loss in yield; the white fly (*Bemisia tabaci*) the European boll-worm (*Heliothis armigera*) and spider mites (*Tetranychus spp.*). Insecticides are used as a preventive method of pest control, as soon as a harmful insect is observed in the crop. The Carbamate granular insecticide Temik is used intensively in the Cukorova region and is used as a standard control method before the 1st or 2nd irrigation early July. Cotton is sown early May and harvested by hand end September, early October.

To demonstrate that good cotton yields can be obtained with a minimum use of insecticides, we set out three demonstration/study experiments in the Cukorova region. Each experiment consisted out of three fields, each of 1-3 ha, with the following treatments; 1) check, so without crop protection, 2) use of insecticides only when really necessary, the IPM method, 3) Use of Temik and then the IPM method, 4) Preventive control as carried out by the farmers.

Field work

Whenever possible Ahmed and myself get out to survey farmer's fields. In the extensive cotton areas I am often under the illusion that I am living in the Middle Ages. Small primitive communities with only rural dirt roads, open stables with the animals with their behind towards the road, the dung everywhere. A place to eat with rough hewn wooden tables and benches, an open fire above which a pot is simmering. We eat bread just out of the fire, beans and yogurt. In the afternoon, in the hot sun sweating and tired from plodding though wet fields and making observations, we quench our thirst with Arian, a kind of local buttermilk, which is sold in small shops along the road. A drink of heaven really nice and refreshing.

Every week we take observations in the study fields with a team of six fellow workers. To work this way with young enthusiastic people is a privilege and a joy. Every morning I am therefore eager to get to work. To get up at 6 o'clock in the morning. It is still cool, but the sun shines. Carefully I open the door of the room of Thomas, but as soon as he sees me he starts jumping in his bed. 'Hi buddy boy', we cuddle and wrestle a bid and then I make toilet and dress. In the meantime Annemiek has laid the breakfast table and then at 7.00 o'clock I leave home, eager to get to work.

Normally I am getting home at 6.00 o'clock in the evening, tired but satisfied. A shower, a little wrestling with Thomas on the floor and then the evening meal. It is then 7.00 o'clock in the evening and already dark. Often I go then to my study to work on a publication about my work of four years in Syria. I strongly feel that I have to make this summary report, although I wrote already the yearly end reports. To be honest, Annemiek is kind of neglected by me, because I am so involved with my work, which really fascinates me. Yes I am a work alcoholic, I have to admit it.

One evening, after a long and exciting day with Ahmed in a far away district, I arrive home at 10.00 o'clock in the evening. Annemiek is not at home. Afraid that something had happened to me she had gone with Thomas to the family of Suzan A., where I find her really upset. We make up but there is the first sign of estrangement and the "drifting apart" continues. Mid-May Annemiek goes with Thomas to the Netherlands to attend the wedding of her sister. The following weeks pass by in a routine of work, eating and sleeping. I am glad when the wife and child are back on station but the relationship is not anymore as it should be.

An important occasion

There is a letter from the FAO representative in Ankara. The director-general of the FAO, Dr. Soama, shall visit Turkey on the 4th of May 1983. I'm requested to be present to meet the big boss. I also receive a telephone call from my direct superior, because he wants to show off his latest project addition and that is me. It is an interesting day. The director-general is an important man and to shake hands with him and to exchange a few words is not the privilege of every FAO employee.

It is fun to see how many assistants there are with the "man" and how severe these helpers and briefcase carriers can look at us field hands, when protocol is not well understood. Even our good old FAO representative is being put to the task. When Dr. Soama jokingly informs me that I have a nice little job ahead of me, I deny this loudly, which causes much laughter and enlightens the tense atmosphere.

A new co-worker

Good news from Rome. An associate expert has been assigned to my project. These are mostly young people, who have just finished their study and in this way can gain practical experience. It is a program, which is funded by the Dutch government. One evening in August there is a knock on our door and there is Ruud v G., my new co-worker. I note already soon that there is a little problem. After a cup of café, small talk with Annemiek and a little play with Thomas, the truth comes out. There are some difficulties with the wife. She is in their hotel room but the door is locked and he is not allowed in. After some encouraging words, an alcoholic reinforcement and the promise that he can sleep here on the couch if the door remains locked, he leaves. The next morning he is waiting with his VW bus in front of the office. Everything is settled. Yes, she was very tired after the long drive from Holland but now she feels much better.

Ruud knows how to get things done. He worked for two years as an associate expert in the Sudan and has driven with his VW bus to Turkey, with wife, daughter and dog. Already soon they have found an apartment and Ruud can start work. Furniture for his apartment he makes himself. Wood working is his hobby and he has brought along a chest with fine woodworking tools. He buys wood and constructs a table, chairs, beds, a couch and cupboards, really nice work. Ruud is also sportive. He played soccer in the Wageningen 1st class club and is soon a respected player in a local team. Yes, it is nice to have a Dutch family living nearby. Rozi, the wife of Ruud and their daughter Dolores, get along well with Annemiek, which results in visits here and there.

A Symposium

Hussein comes over for a visit. He is very busy to organize a symposium on IPM on cotton. It has been decided that this happening will take place in Adana on 5 – 9 September 1983. This means that Ahmed and I shall be host. There will be representatives from Sudan, Pakistan, Syria, Jordan, England and the four cotton regions of Turkey. The governor of the province Adana shall open the symposium and also the FAO representative shall say a few words. It promises to be a busy and interesting day in which we, the FAO staff shall play a leading role.

The representatives arrive and are accommodated in hotels. I get acquainted with the colleagues from Sudan and Pakistan, greet old friends of Syria and get to know the Turkish colleagues of Achmed. Also Hussein arrives, harried and somewhat tense but also full of good cheer; it is still his symposium, he is the boss man. However the program develops differently than he has foreseen.

That day I leave home for the conference hall at 6.45 o'clock, to check, together with Ahmed if everything with regard to logistics is arranged. Service, café, thee, the lunch, all those modules have to be in place. Hussein is not there yet and that is strange, because normally he is very punctual. The participants arrive and everybody sits down. The governor enters and is welcomed by Ahmed, his director and myself. He is guest of honor and shall open the symposium.

Now we are waiting for Hussein and I am getting worried.

We are already fifteen minutes over time., when Annemiek enters. It was agreed that she would attend the meeting as a listener. She signals Achmed and me and tells that Hussein arrived at our apartment at 10 minutes past 7.00 o'clock in high distress, because he could not pass water anymore. She, Annemiek has taken him in our car to the hospital and there he stays at the moment. I have now to take charge and open the symposium; everything goes as planned.

Then I have to finalize the financial arrangements; the allowances for hotel and travel costs. This is quite a bit of work, but the participants are satisfied and I am relieved, a job well done. Now we can give full attention to Hussein. We visit him in the hospital and on the day when the operation is going to take place I accompany him to the operation room. A few days later we say good bye. By way of Ankara he shall fly to Amman, Jordan. I request Ruud to accompany him as far as Ankara and to make sure that he gets on the plane to Amman without a problem. We are getting back to normal; well that is not entirely true.

The separation, the end and a new beginning.

Then there is the split between us. Annemiek and Thomas are going back to Holland early October. It is an escape. I follow a month later to take leave. Annemiek and Thomas stay with her parents. I get a room with her brother Bert, with whom I get along well but who does not really understand what it is all about. There are no arguments or reproaches, but more a realization that it is over and that our life expectancies are not in agreement. Moreover there is Thomas, my first concern. Annemiek makes the decision; she wants to separate.

Before my return to Turkey I arrange with the assistance of brother Marc, a solicitor, whose advice; of wanting to settle the separation in harmony, appeals to me. I don't want to burden the relation unnecessary in this very sensitive stage, with regard to the future of Thomas. Early December '83, I fly back to Turkey and have a lonely and cold Christmas in the flat in Adana.

Then there is another big disappointment. I receive a message that the project is not going to be extended, because UNEP does not longer want to finance the program. So I am requested to close down the project and that I am expected in Rome by the end of February '84. I have now two very busy months ahead of me. Furniture and linen I can sell in Adana, there are enough buyers. My private car I sell at a good price in Ankara. Most of our belongings I send to Annemiek in Holland, so that she can start with her new life with Thomas.

And then our adventure in Turkey is over. I could not realize our objectives here. The hope that the Turkisch colleagues could continue the work is not being realized. The pesticide lobby in the Cukorova region is very powerful and there is much money involved. The concept IPM is a direct threat to a very profitable business.

One morning Ahmed informs me kind of shamefaced that he has accepted a job with a chemical company. He becomes the sales manager for the product Temik, the Carbonate granular insecticide. 'Pieter, I received a tremendous offer, which I simply could not refuse. We really need the money and the Government hardly pays.' It is not up to me to criticize. I know that it has been a very difficult decision for him. For me it is a great disappointment, but I wish him all the best for the future.

I get a strong impression that in FAO circles, one is already aware of my misfortune. The FAO representative in Ankara wishes me good luck when I say goodbye. At head office in Rome I get an offer to participate in an evaluation mission on cotton in the Sudan, however I decline the work.

There is the separation to cope with and how to get my life in balance again. All this requires much energy. In first instance the chief does not understand that I refuse this appointment, because to work for the organization is very special, but when I explain my reasoning he understands.After rain comes sunshine is the saying and that is certainly true for me. I receive a message from the FAO that Pakistan wants me as a FAO expert for a new to start IPM cotton project in Sind province.

Syrian women in new year dresses

Syria, nomad

Syria sheep market

Turkey, in the field

Turkey, village life

Turkey, field workers

Purified by work in
Pakistan (1985 – 1987)

The beginning

I am again a free man. The separation is concluded satisfactory. That Christmas 1984 I stay with mother and there are visits with the brothers and their families. During the old and new year festivities I stay with my sister Maartje and her family in Uitwellingerga. I am looking forward to my travel to Pakistan and my new assignment there. Several colleagues want to meet with me. Dr Derek C. of the ODA has requested the FAO that I visit with him at the ODA office in England, so as to discuss cooperation between our two programs in Pakistan. Then there is an invitation of Dr Dan G., professor of the university of Tel Aviv, Israel. He is very much interested in my work in Syria. My travel itinerary to Pakistan is therefore as follows: On the 8th of January 1985 I fly to London, where I shall be the guest of Derek for two days. Then to Rome for a briefing at FAO headquarters and from there to Israel. Here I shall stay for one week and then I fly to Karachi, Pakistan.

I say goodbye to the family. That last evening in Gorssel I spend drinking till the early morning with house mate Piet D. and Frans, my landlord and his wife Tineke. Everything is packed, because the following morning at 5.00 o'clock I shall travel by taxi to Deventer, to take the first train to Amsterdam and from there by bus to Schiphol airport. That morning at 5.00 o'clock Frank knocks on my door, because the taxi is waiting. I dress quickly and with luggage and all I stumble down the stairs into the cold, after a last greeting to Frans and Piet.

My visits to London, Rome and Israel go by as planned and on 21st January 1985, in the morning I land in Karachi. Here I am met by a representative of the Pakistan Central Cotton Committee (PCCC), who drives me to the office. Here I meet first mr. Ahmed, the secretary of the PCCC and the right hand man of the vice president, whom I shall meet that afternoon. I check in the hotel where a room has been reserved for me. I take lunch and a quick rest, with the alarm clock on stand bye. Then it is back to the office for the meeting with the vice president of the PCCC, Dr, Hishhamul H. . whom I met for the first time in Turkey. He is glad to see me and together we drink thee and I tell him about my experiences in Syria and Turkey. The next day I fly to Islamabad. Here the offices of the UNDP and FAO are located, and where the logistic details for my stay in Pakistan are finalized. I am introduced to the UNDP Chargé d'Affairs for Pakistan and the FAO representative and register myself with the Dutch Embassy. In the UNDP office I meet with a quite wild looking colleague, Dr. Jan M., who appears to be the father of an old Deventer student friend of mine. Also very special, by arrival at the airport of Islamabad, I walk almost in the way of Mr. Hans van den Broek, our minister of foreign affairs, who has just arrived for an official visit to Pakistan. That evening, Jan, his wife and me stand in the lift of our hotel with him and there is polite conversation; Dutchmen together in a new world.

Karachi is an entirely new experience, a very busy town,

hot with a cacophony of noise and with people almost identically dressed in tin cotton balloon trousers and long light colored cotton shirts, which reach till the knees. I stay in the Beach hotel Karachi, which is not far from the PCCC office. It is a colonial type of building with broad verandas and high ceilings. It is located close by the harbor, so that takes care of a nice sea breeze. I feel myself at home here and shall always stay in this hotel during visits to Karachi.

The FAO cotton project is affiliated with the PCCC, a sub-department of the Ministry of Agriculture. The head office is located in Karachi and there are two experimental stations; one near the town Multan in the Punjab province and the other one near the village Sakrand in the province Sindh. The FAO project has a complement of four specialists; the project manager, who is stationed at the head office in Karachi, the IPM expert, me, shall be working in Sakrand and an extension specialists and a mechanization expert will be stationed in Multan. The four of us have different nationalities. The project manager, Mike W. is an Englishman, the extension specialist, Boonlert S., comes from Thailand and the mechanization man, Padolino, is a Pilipino national. And yes, I am a Dutchman, who over the years has become an expert on IPM.

Work program

Also in Pakistan cotton is an important cash crop and offers employment to millions of people. In the Punjab and Sindh were respectively 1.746.000 and 617.000 ha cotton cultivated in 1985. Planting takes place from mid April till early June. Harvesting is carried out by hand and takes place in Sindh from late August till early November and in the Punjab during November and December.

My plan of work consists of many objectives. The main

purpose is to introduce the concept of IPM in the Sindh province, with all its relevant inputs such as; proper sampling of the different insect species, the recognition of insect pests, predators and parasites and their relevant population dynamics in cotton and very important to establish economic injury levels (EIL) for the most important insect pest species. Also very important is the training of national scientists in entomological field work and this is quite exhausting by temperatures over 35 degrees C. During our field work it appears that the spiny bollworm (*Earias sp.*) is the most serious pest insect in cotton in Sindh. (7) Also observed are the white fly (*Bemisia sp.*), mites (*Tetranychus sp.*), the pink bollworm (*Pectinophora gosypiella*) and planthoppers (*Cicadellidae*). We also find many predators such as lady beetles (*Coccinellidae*), predator mirids (*Reduvidae, Anthocoridae*) and spiders (*Arachnidae*).

Working with the young people is a challenge and also very rewarding. I get up at 5.00 o'clock in the morning, because we want to be in the field at 6.00 o'clock to start with the observations in the several experiments. At 10.00 o'clock it is already very warm and in the afternoon it is over 40 degrees. Therefore we always try to finish with the field work early afternoon. Then it is back to the office to do some administrative work, one hour rest and then at 5.00 o'clock in the afternoon we do some sport; some running in the fields or playing badminton with the lads.

Day to day affairs

I am the first FAO expert who has arrived but there is already a FAO consultant at work. Jack S. is an old FAO hand, who has worked many years as a cotton plant breeder in Pakistan. Jack is an old gnarled Englishman, who has as terms of reference; to order the necessary materials and to organize the FAO office before the FAO staff arrives. For the Karachi office Jack has already drawn up a list of requirements. The official orders for FAO head office are typed up and signed by me, because Jack as a consultant is not allowed to sign, he can only give advice.

Together with Jack I visit the experimental station Sakrand, my future workstation for the coming two years. It is a rainy miserable day early February and the station looks abandoned. We are welcomed by Dr. Barkat S.,the director of the station. We drink sweetened thee with much milk, which warms us and makes me feel better. My first impression of my future place of work is not directly favorable. I meet the staff of the entomological department, young people with whom it will be nice to work. The head of the department, Dr Baloch, is for study in Germany and shall only return next year. I soon discover that the laboratory needs to be completely equipped and together with the men I make a list of essentials, which have to be ordered. Also the other departments; plant diseases, plant breeding, and soil give their requirements. Also agricultural equipment is urgently needed. The next morning the sun shines and we drive back to Karachi. It is the start of a very busy time.

In those days the PCCC Karachi is a place with much activity. Dr Hisham is a dynamic man, who has worked hard to realize projects with the FAO and ODA. Two rooms are assigned to our FAO project, which we fit out as our office. Jack works fast and he stayed for many years in Pakistan. He knows people and he has soon engaged a secretary, whom he knows from his time in Multan. There is a large budget for cars and other materials and the instructions from head office are to spend the money as quickly as possible. Jack keeps on writing orders. Cars keep on arriving and for Sakrand there is a Toyota land cruiser and a Toyota Corolla sedan. According to FAO rules I am not allowed to use a project car for private use., so I order for myself a Toyota Corolla station, which I can import as a UN staff member without paying import duty. It is my first completely new car and I am real proud when the car is parked in all its glory in front of the office.

Colleagues arrive, as well as for our project as for the ODA. Also my project manager, Mike W., is now on station. He is my age and we work well together. Soon there is a work routine. I stay ten days in Sakrand. Then on Friday I come to Karachi and work that day in the office with Mike. In the weekend I look up friends and visit the Karachi Yacht club of which I have become a member. On Monday morning I drive then back to Sakrand in the interior. It is a nice way to combine work with social activities. After work we often gather with several staff members to play badminton or I go running in the fields of the station. Then in the evening I am mostly alone. I have a house boy, who cooks for me and keeps the place tidy. After dinner I watch some TV. It is very quiet outside. The typical Pakistan music has a mystic appeal for me. It is relaxing and very suitable in the heat of the night.

After the emotional year 1984, during which the separation took much of my energy, my present life rhythm is refreshing and healing. There is that routine of rising early, the field work, the processing of data, the relaxation in the evening and the absolute silence of the night. When I stay in Sakrand during the Saturday and Sunday I often visit the Franciscan missionaries, who live in the town Newabshah. The friars Tom and Victor are always glad to see me. We eat together a simple meal and talk about our work during the past weeks. Then in the early afternoon Tom and Victor take a nap and I drive back to Sakrand. Tom and Victor work with the most destitute people in their community. Through them I obtain a good reliable driver and also good workmen when we construct a barn at the station to house all the new farm machinery It is strange and also frustrating but Dr.Barakat and the other colleagues do not have any experience to find trades men in their community.

The women in Sindh

I feel at home in Sind. I learn a few hundred words in Urdu. There are discussions about women and marriage, which can only take place between friends. When I meet one afternoon the wife and two daughters of Barakat, they dressed in black with veils before their faces. I covers quasi frightened my face with my hand, which causes much giggling from her and daughters. 'He Kalroo' I say one evening to my senior co-worker, 'how does your wife like it to always have to walk a few paces behind you, to have to cover her face and to ask your permission for everything she wants to do'? Kalroo is honest and replies 'now really she is not directly enthusiastic about this state of affairs, but it is a fact of life and cannot be changed'. Yusuf, another co-worker is going to marry his niece. Yes, he finds that the man is the head in a marriage and if he wants something then that is the way it is going to be. On the way with a group of extension workers I ask the men if they want to come back as a woman in another life. The men at first look kind of stunned, but then one of them starts to laugh. 'No way', but then he adds 'we are Muslims, we do not believe in reincarnation, ha, ha, ha'. In the interior of Sind it is normal that one marries in the family. Marriages between nieces and nephews are very normal and are arranged at an early age of the children. In that way the clan remains strong. In theory every Muslim man may marry with four women, however in practice this can cause problems. Our Barakat married already very young with his niece and they have six children. The family lives in Sakrand.

He studied plant breeding for six years in Canada, travelled much and is familiar with the Western ways with regard to marriage and standing of women. In Pakistan however he is a Sindi through and through and likes the idea of several wifes just for him. In the head office in Karachi I hear rumors with regard to a nice big woman who works in the office. One afternoon I come back from the field and till my surprise I see Barakat sitting in the garden. He looks very depressed with dark circles under his eyes and you can see that he is in trouble. After a few pats on the back, there is a tear and out comes the story. Mrs Barakat has told him to get lost, he is not welcome in the house anymore. She is very angry because he is married again in Karachi. 'You mean that big ... '? Barakat nods, she alone ... he is a man, what could he do? After some time there is peace again and Barakat has another responsibility.

The unofficial rulers of Sindh

Sindh is a somewhat backward province. There is much difference in the way of living between Karachi and this province. In Sind there exists a feudal system. Rich landowners (*samadari's*) possess thousands ha land and have often their own private armies. Thousands of little farmers are completely dependent on them and really are a kind of serf. The word of the *samadari* is law. You can easily recognize them in their long white robes and head dress, round, smooth, well fed faces and a very relaxed manner of movement. Sindh has a reputation. Not every Karachi inhabitant finds himself safe in Sind. There are criminals (*decoys*), who sometimes kidnap well to do people and that gives the area a somewhat notorious reputation. Barakat assures me that I do not have to worry. The experiment station and its people and certainly me, as a very valued co-worker, are under the protection of

a very important *samadari*. One afternoon we pay him a
visit. It is an interesting meeting. The man speaks excellent
English, has studies abroad and knows what it is all about.
There is another unusual meeting with the unofficial kings
of Sindh. One evening Barakat invites me for a social evening
with several *samadari's* . It is an experience. We sit in easy
chairs round a campfire. It is still very warm. That day it was
50 degrees C. There is small talk and people smoke. There is
also a kind of drink in a large scale out of which everybody
regularly takes a full cup to drink. Barakat encourages me to
try the brew. It is a kind of herb drink laced with hash hish
and it is very good against the heat. It slows people down. I refuse politely, because I want to remain clear headed. However
I understand that this brew in these surroundings is accept-
able. It relaxes people in a very hot and demanding climate.

There is also a national movement "Sindh for the Sindhi's".
Every true blood Sindhi is a member and of course also
Barakat and his people of the station. One Saturday there
will be a large meeting near the village Sun, which is situated on the bank of the Indus river. Barakat asks if I like to
come along. The leader of the movement, an old sheikh, not
very well regarded by the Government, shall be present and
address his followers. That morning we start early. We drive
through kilometers of foreland of the Indus river to the river
bank where we leave the car. In the company of many men,
wearing the traditional Sindhi cap, many armed with hunting
rifles, loaded with solid shot, knifes and pistols hidden under
waist coats and robes, we cross the river in boats to the village. It is a happening of significance. I sit between hundreds
of men and we listen to the "big man". The village Sun is a
hamlet which can be placed in antiquity. Century old walls,
narrow streets, I am transported into the past. The next week
I am in Karachi and Dr Hisham asks me if I am going to be

in politics. My presence at the meeting in Sun has been noted in Islamabad and has been investigated. Mike warns me to be careful. It seems that my presence there has made an impression. 'Mike' I say, 'Í live and work there, every day I meet and socialize with these people: of course I want to learn and understand their way of life. In that way I earn their respect and confidence and will they listen to me. We want to accomplish there something, now'?

Socializing

I want to meet people outside my field of work. From a colleague I learn that there is a large UN project going on near the town Hydrabad. They are building there an Institute for training air traffic controllers, under guidance of some UN experts. Hydrabad is situated on my way to Karachi. One morning I decide to pass by, so as to meet the UN collegues who work there. I meet Brian J., the project manager, an Australian in his sixties and an expert on radar. There is café, good talk and it appears that we both like sailing. Brian is a member of the Karachi Yacht club. 'Tomorrow, Saturday, I shall collect you at the Beach hotel and then I shall introduce you in the Yacht club' says Brian, 'and in the evening you have dinner with us and then you can meet my wife Pamela and daughter Rosie'. This cordiality and hospitability, it makes me feel wanted. I am glad that I made the effort to visit with my UN colleague in Hydrabad. That Saturday I become a member of the Yacht club, crew for Brian in his boat and have a tremendous weekend. Every Sunday afternoon there is a sailing race between the members of the club. It is a mixed company, which consists of well to do Pakistani nationals and foreigners of several nationalities. In the summer months, the monsoon season, we sail in the harbor of Karachi between the there located sea ships. In the winter months, when the sea is not too rough, we sail at sea before the coast and that is beautiful sailing. I soon buy a Karachi dinghy of a young English banker, who is going to leave the country. I have much fun with my boat. Every two weeks with the sailing and the interaction with the members of the club I can recharge my mental batteries and then return refreshed to the interior of Sindh.

Hard work of a Franciscan friar

An experience which makes a deep impression on me. During a visit to Victor and Tom in Newabshah, the latter tells me that he wants to show me something. We make an appointment and one Saturday we drive together to a location on the bank of the Indus river. There in the distance on the foreland of the river there is a kind of a terp on which there is a village. From the bank of the river till the village we see a row of concrete telephone poles, between which hangs a big electric cable. In that village on that terp in the middle of that foreland of the Indus lives a small community of Christians. Tom recounts proudly that a brother Franciscan has lobbied for years with the government to realize electric power for this community in the outback. I am really impressed: To realize in a Muslim country, with a kind of primitive admin- istration system, this commodity for an ethnical minority is really something, a work of utmost patience and love. We visit the village and meet with the people. There works an electric pump, which provides water for their vegetable gardens and there is electric light. Here is done, very quietly, much import- ant work, again a lesson of life for me.

End of a period

End March 1987. I am going to leave Pakistan. My contract

period is over and I am going back to the Netherlands. I say goodbye to friends and acquaintances. I sell my car to another Dutchman but for my boat I have no buyer so I donate it to the Karachi Yacht club. My time in Pakistan has been a productive and healing period.

To meet again in Pakistan (1995)

During my stay in Somalia end 1994, under contract by the Dutch government, I receive a request of an American company, to participate in a project in Pakistan. The Winrock International Institute for Agricultural Development has made an agreement with the Directorate General Agriculture Research for the province of Sindh, Pakistan.

The National Commission on Agriculture in its 1988 report was optimistic for the future of cotton growing. However as critical was identified the absence of proper plant protection practices. The commission suggested the formation of an IPM department at Tandojam, Sindh. This recommendation was strongly supported by the World Bank, which funded a five year master plan (1988 – 2000) of the National Agricultural Research Centre (NARC), which placed priority on IPM practices to achieve the maximum potential of field crops. Winrock International was funded by the World Bank to assist with the implementation of this program in Sindh province.

Terms of reference

My main objective is, in close collaboration with national scientists, to develop a draft proposal for a five year cotton IPM research and development program for Sindh. And then, to design and implement a cotton IPM research program for the 1995/96 season. This means;

- Prepare recommendations to update existing economic threshold levels (ETL's) for the major cotton insect pests,
- Prepare a field manual; a pictorial guide for harmful and beneficial insects on cotton in Sindh, (8)
- Train research workers in different techniques of IPM, like sampling and the recognition of insect pests, predators and parasites,
- To hold workshops for extension workers and leading farmers, to further introduce the concept of IPM.

It is for me a contract for six months, starting April 1995. This is for me a nice program, tailor made for me. I inform Winrock that I am available as soon as my contract in Somalia is finished.

Winrock International

Winrock is an American rural development organization, which is not familiar to me. Before I get to work for them in Pakistan, I like to get to know the people in their head office in Arkansas. My visit is agreed upon and on 6 March I fly from Schiphol to Little Rock Arkansas where we land in the evening. I am met by a representative of Winrock and we drive to the head office. It is a kind of a campus with several office buildings, ware houses and guest houses, situated on a large piece of land situated outside Little Rock. It is already late and I am brought directly to a guest house. In the morning I shall meet the research staff in charge of the Pakistan program

Henk K. is the program director of the Pakistan project.

He is naturalized American, originally from the Netherlands and with him I discuss my work responsibilities in Pakistan. I take care of a presentation of my stay in Somalia for the senior management. I also study the background of the NARC master plan, 1988 – 2000 for the province of Sindh. Dan C., my old professor at LSU, now lives in Arkansas. I inform him that I am visiting with Winrock and he comes over for a visit. I stay one night with him and his wife Gerrie at their place and it is a pleasure to reminisce with him about times in the past. I use my time in the USA. On the 10 of March I fly to Baton Rouge and stay there with Joe and Anne. There is a get together with Willem and Bien K. and other friends of my time in Louisiana and then on the 17 of March I fly back to the Netherlands. Then two weeks of preparations and saying goodbyes to family and friends and then on 4 April 1995 I fly from Schiphol to Karachi.

The office of Winrock in Pakistan is located in Hydrabad and I arrive there at 6.00 o'clock in the morning. I meet Dr Taki U., the team leader and together we take breakfast. I sleep for a few hours and then in the afternoon I meet, together with Taki, Mr. Makdoom, the secretary of the Sindh Agricultural Research Corporation. He knows me from the past and tells me 'yes we have specially asked for you and I am glad to welcome you back'. As part of the Agriculture Research Institute the IPM Institute Sindh has been established and this will be my place of work. My direct co-worker will be Mr. Buriro, the senior entomologist, and an old acquaintance. There is a hearty welcome with back slapping here and there. Buriro was in the past a minor official but now he is "boss" and 'Dr. Pieter we are going to work very hard'. I suggest that we also work closely together with the Federal Cotton Research Institute in Sakrand, where I worked formerly as a FAO expert. It is very nice to meet my friends there again and it is agreed that we shall work closely together. This cooperation is important. National and regional programs should work together in developing agricultural policies, otherwise there shall be no lasting results.

Work program

My objectives for the coming six months consist of two units: First, to carry out an IPM program in Sindh for the season 1995/1996. Secondly, to develop a five year IPM program on cotton in Sindh. The work plan for the coming season consists of three modules; a) research, b) training and c) information. The IPM institute has seven workers, who are full time engaged in the program. The research entails the sampling of insect pests and beneficial insects, the establishment of ETL's, to set up an insect collection and to rear insects in the laboratory. The training consists here in that the staff are directly participating in all aspects of the work. Furthermore we organize several workshops for agricultural extension workers. The information module entails the making of a reference booklet with pictures and descriptions of several harmful and beneficial insects and descriptions of the several ways of sampling the different insect species. My second task; the design of a five year IPM program for cotton is quite some work. It consists of seven parts; research, training, extension, a demonstration program, personnel, materials and a budget.

Day to day affairs

It are six busy but also very nice months and I am in hog heaven. I work well with Taki the manager and with café at hand there is much laughter when we are working with our computers next to each other in the office. Winrock has rented a large house, which serves as an office but also as a guest house for the temporary staff. There is also domestic personnel, who cooks and washes for us. It is the intention that Gerda also comes to Pakistan but first she goes for a fortnight to America to visit with Joe and Anne. Due to family circumstances she could not come with me during my visit in March. Gerda arrives mid June in Pakistan and she is an asset to our small community. She gets to know the several National and International colleagues and attends several workshops. Together with Doris, the wife of Taki, they visit the market to buy the necessary vegetables and eats for the household. However there develops a tumor in her belly and we decide that she goes back to the Netherlands for more research. It appears that an operation is necessary, which takes place in the hospital in Vlissingen on the 20th July 1995. The next week I fly to the Netherlands to be with her. The operation is a complete success and the first week of August I fly back to Pakistan to finalize my assignment, which ends early October.

Pakistan, Sakrant photo session

Pakistan, Sind farmers

Hard and good times in the Sudan (1987 – 1992)

Stay in the Netherlands

Early April 1987, after a long absence I am back in the Netherlands. There is again a period of rest and new acquaintances. In the rest house of my mother there is no guest room available for a longer period of time. The house of the family Z., where I rented a room two years ago, is gone, completely wiped out by a fire in May 1985. There stands now the post office of the village. It is a strange feeling; that what was is no more.. That brief period of the past, those nice months I spend there; in the morning drinking café with Piet D., discussing the papers we were writing; now only a remembrance.

One afternoon, when I walk along the main street, someone shouts my name and there stands suddenly Lamie G. in front of me.I remember him as a timid rather insecure young man, in the Deventer student fraternity. Now I see a big set man, who appears to be very happy to see me. We shake hands, there is a mighty blow on my shoulders and he invites for dinner at his place. There I meet Nienke his wife, admire baby daughter and I have to tell about past experiences. Lamie has had his ups and downs and often made life somewhat difficult for himself. He is a kind of free living soul and does not like the bureaucratic rules of society. He is busy to build by himself an extension to his house without a permit and he does not care what might happen in the future to this work of freedom.

Things are happening. Nienke has an aunt, who perhaps has a little house for rent. In the past it was a farm barn, which was transformed into an apartment with a living room, two small bed rooms, a bath room and a small kitchen. The whole hovel looks kind of shabby with old antiquated furniture and worn-out carpet, gas fire and dust everywhere. However, for me it is an excellent temporary accommodation. I file a petition for a telephone connection, buy some kitchen utensils and prepare for the first time in years my own dinners.

I draw up the balance of my present circumstance and my wish for the future. I am now ready for a new relationship and there is a correspondence with a certain Gerda Bliek, who lives in the province Zeeland. There is an invitation for a visit to her home in her village on the Walcheren peninsula. With regard to transport I have made progress. I exchanged my Jawa 350 cc motorbike, bought secondhand in 1984, for a new BMW 800 cc motorcycle by a dealer in Apeldoorn and with this bike I explore the country, a real pleasure.

Early August I ride with my pride to Zeeland. It will be my first visit to this province. My destination is the hamlet Kleverskerke, near the village Arnemuiden. I enter the main street, give gas and I am out of the hamlet before I can say "yes". Number 23 appears to be a house like a palace. Kind of intimidated I park the bike in front of this imposing building and shyly I ring the bell. The lady who opens the door is someone to behold. Nice big arms, beautiful dress and she does not say much. I am allowed to enter and she walks directly to the kitchen and leaves me alone in the vestibule, where I remove my motor dressing. Much later Gerda tells everybody, who is interested, that my soccer stockings, army boots, dirty trousers and antiquated sweater, made a big impression on her; pure nature. There is an immediate rapport; no tension, mutual feelings develop naturally, because there is much in common. Gerda is a widow of an entrepreneur pure sang, who died too young. She comes from a large close knit family with deep roots in Zeeland, in balance and with the silent wish to work in Africa.

Those first get-togethers with our mutual families are funny. One weekend, never to be forgotten, I am allowed to stay over. It is really a happening in that little hamlet with the parents and a married sister with children next door and other family close by in Arnemuiden. That Sunday morning I meet the eldest brother for the first time. He is kind of heavy in his Christian conviction and in his black suit, straight out of church it means getting used to for both sides.

On another occasion we visit sister, brother in law and their two daughters, who live opposite the street. I meet several family members, all very curious and I learn to listen to rural Zeeuws language. Of course I reply but then in my rural dialect of my town Deventer. In the village Hemelum in the province Friesland, where my family has a summer cottage, Gerda meets my family. Mother is directly in love with her, very glad that the son, always on the go, is at long last going to be homely again. With my sister Maartje it is also soon "old girls current loaf". The brother are quite happy to know that the "man" has found at long last a nice woman.

Getting to work

There is a job offer from the FAO. The project "Development and Application of IPM on Cotton in the Sudan" has to be evaluated. The Dutch government, which is funding this project, wants to know why IPM has not yet been accepted by

the Government of the Sudan, while the project started in
1979. The Netherlands want to know if it serves a purpose to
continue with this program. If I am interested?! Of course I
say yes. IPM on cotton is my specialty; the problem of cotton
plant protection in the Sudan is well known in professional
circles. So it is a very interesting assignment, right up my
street. The work will take about three weeks, starting end
March. The mission will consist out of three men; a representative of the Dutch Government, The FAO mission leader,
that is me, and a representative of the Government of Sudan.

There is in Rome the necessary technical briefing and logistics. After having visited many offices, my travel itinerary
is organized and I am familiar with the objectives of the work.
Then on 18 of March '87 I fly to Amsterdam. That week I stay
with mother in a guest room of her rest house in Gorssel,
where she lives. I visit with family and friends and then on
26 of March I fly to the Sudan.

The mission

Arrival in Sudan, where I disembark in Kartoum. I am
met by a representative of the national FAO office. I meet
with the FAO representative for Sudan and visit the Dutch
embassy, where I meet the agricultural attaché, Pim P., who
shall participate in the mission as the representative of the
Dutch Government. At the faculty Entomology of the university of Khartoum, I meet my third team member, Dr. Sayed
El B., a tall pleasant man, whom I like straight away.

It are ten very busy days. The Agricultural Research
Corporation of Sudan (ARC), the institute to which the project is connected, is located in Wad Medani. This town is
situated at the Blue Nile, about 100 km South of Khartoum.
There are in depth talks with Dr Badar M., the FAO expert,
and the national coordinator of the project, Dr. Assim A. .

We also talk with national scientists and the management of the Gezira and Rahad schemes. It is the overall opinion that the present way of plant protection in cotton is not effective and that the concept of IPM has to be tried. With regard to good results in this direction during the past season we can conclude that the project can be extended for a start for one more year.

In Wad Medani I stay at the Gezira club, a building out of the period that the English governed the country. It is a building with high ceilings and large ceiling fans and mosquito nets around the beds and of course no air conditioning. The rooms are kind of dusty, due to the many gaps in walls and shutter, but it is adequate for me.

Badar has rented here a room for a longer period and he is a good host. He is an American, originally from Pakistan, and has as specialty; biological control of insect pests. In the evening, after work the team discusses the day's experiences over a beer or something stronger, organized by Pim, who has his connections. In Khartoum I stay at the Acropole hotel, owned by a Greek family. George P. and his brothers are host to many expatriates, who stay in the Sudan for some time. The hotel is clean, the food simple but good and the prices are reasonable. The family has also a hotel on the Greek island Corfu and every six months the brothers rotate between Khartoum and Corfu. The family works already more than fifty years in Sudan and started with this hotel in 1955.

The months of spring 1987 are beautiful indeed, with prospects of work and a social life with a very nice lady. I am eligible to manage the cotton project in the Sudan. Mid September I learn that my appointment as Chief Techncal Advisor (CTA) has been confirmed and a very busy period starts. Gerda appears to be a tremendous asset. It is a new and special experience for me to have someone assists in a practical manner with selecting and buying all kinds of gear. In the past, on all my travels abroad, I always had to manage everything by myself. Household goods are packed. IKEA furniture is bought, the transport arranged with a logistics specialist in Wageningen. There are talks with the colleagues of the University of Wageningen, They are the representatives of the Ministry of Foreign Affairs, department Development Assistance, which is funding the project. And then there are the very pleasant farewell visits with family and friends, during which many a glass is enjoyed.

The Beginning

Mid October 1987 I fly to Rome for the final instructions at FAO headquarters and then I travel to the Sudan. Gerda shall visit with me for two weeks during Christmas and New Year and that is something to look forward to. To start again with a new assignment in a less developed country is not always easy and often causes a so-called *"Blue Period"* (hell, why did I start with this ...).

This project in this country is now not directly a sinecure. Right from the start in November 1979 already eleven FAO experts have slaved away here. The cooperation of national scientists was not directly enthusiastic, especially in the early beginning., due to the fact that the chemical industry funded most research programs. The first phase of the project started in 1979 and ran till 1984. I am the second CTA in the next phase, which started in 1985. Badar is the bio-control specialist. Ahmed A. is the agriculture extension specialist who arrives two months after me.

The Work Program

Cotton cultivation is important for the economy of Sudan.

Archaeolic findings suggest that cotton was already cultivated in 50 BC. It is planted in July/August and harvested during February/March. The Gezira and Rahad regions are the two most important irrigated agricultural areas of Sudan. The Gezira has approximately 840.000 ha under cultivation of which 200.000 ha are planted under cotton in rotation with wheat, sorghum, peanuts and a fallow period. The Rahad region consists of 125.000 ha of which 50.000 ha are planted in cotton in rotation with sorghum and peanuts and a fallow. Each region is managed by a central administration, which is responsible to the Ministry of Agriculture. The region is arranged in sub divisions, which are directed by agricultural managers. They are responsible for all agricultural practices, including the use of pesticides. Insecticides are applied by agricultural planes.

The objectives of the project can be described as follows; developing and testing IPM practices and extending them to the cotton regions. Our research is concentrated on two important modules of this concept, namely;1) to make use of the natural enemies of the three most important pest species; aphids (*Aphis sp.*), bollworms (*Heliothis sp.*) and the white fly (*Bemisia sp*), 2) to increase the ETL,s for these insect pests in cotton.

This strategy means that insecticides should only be used when absolutely necessary, so that natural enemies have a better chance to control the harmful insects. The ultimate objective is to convince the management of the agricultural schemes that a preventive use of insecticides is not necessary to secure good harvests. It results in high production costs and can affect the quality of the cotton lint.

In order to obtain satisfactory results, much tedious and tiring field work is necessary. It means long days in the field from August till February. Every week we sample the different

harmful and beneficial insect species in the different experimental fields. Plant development is monitored. For this all
fruiting forms; fruits, flowers and flower buds are counted in
a sample of cotton plants. When the cotton is harvested, the
yield is weighed and the quality of the lint established.

Daily Affairs

Those first few months after arrival are not the easiest
ones, because there is not directly an exuberant welcome. It
starts on the road from Khartoum to Wad Medani. On the
way we make a stop near a resting place to drink something.
A car stops in front of us and out steps Dr Osman G., the director of the ARC. He is rather surprised and not too thrilled
to see me. I am getting the impression that decisions have
been made in his absence, with which he is not in accordance
for one or another dubious reason. Here is a man, who is not
a supporter of our project.

In Wad Medani I stay at first in the Gezira club, where Dr
Badar takes care of me. I meet other expatriates and start
looking for a house. I have no intention to stay in the Gezira
club during my entire stay in the Sudan. In the ARC I also get
to know better my national colleagues and the director of the
IPM project, Dr Assim, whom I have met on previous occasions. Assim has already worked for seven years with foreign
specialists on IPM and he is a convinced participant. He is
quiet, somewhat reserved but he appears to be a good professional colleague. Most of the scientists of the ARC have studied in England or America and completed there a PhD. They
are well qualified and have published in scientific journals.

The office of the CTA has not been used for the past two
years. Badar has his own work place and has not made use
of the room. When I unlock the door of my new office, a stale
air assails me and I am confronted with a huge heap of paper

laying around. It takes me a day to clean out the room and to create a place where I can work.

Work

Slowly the CTA room becomes my office with all the maps and folders in the right place. It is the start of a busy period. Experiments are being laid out and are sampled at weekly intervals. You get up at 4.30 am in the morning, when it is still dark and cool. We assemble at the ARC. Assim has a team of six fieldworkers and a headman and with them I go into the fields each morning. The ferocious sunshine and midday heat don't invite for work in the fields in the afternoon. There is a fixed routine. At 5.00 o'clock we drive with the truck to the fields, a ride of about half an hour. In the field everyone has his task. I sample the plants with my sweep net for flying insects. Then when the work has been done, around noon, it is good to rest and the men have their lunch.

There is for me more work to be done. The maintenance of the cars is important and also the task to secure petrol and gasoline on a regular basis is a constant headache. In Wad Medani there is no car repair shop, which can carry out proper maintenance of the cars. For this we have to go to Khartoum, but also here the facilities are scarce. However we are in luck. A Dutch entrepreneur and adventurer has established in the periphery of Khartoum an extensive car maintenance establishment. He was able to come to an agreement with the Government and has driven to the Sudan through the dessert. When I arrive at the work place for the first time at 10.0 o'clock in the morning I am really amazed what I see. Willem T., the boss has a team of six co-workers, who are just very busy drinking café. They all look kind of rough and suddenly I like to be *"Charles of current whip"*. 'Good morning gentlemen 'I say 'Í beg pardon but I like to converse with your director'. This in the dialect of the town The Hague, which is famous in the Netherlands for its snotty accent. I really enjoy their reaction. They look kind of cross eyed and then try to ignore me. Later on we get on real well when I talk normal; the language of my province Zeeland in the Netherlands.

I make my acquaintance with Willem and I know that I have seen him years ago on television. He had at that time organized a food transport to Polen and with the emotional shout 'and we are going to Polen ' the convoy of trucks started to move. It is a pleasure to meet this hotshot, because what he again has organized here in Khartoum has my respect and admiration. Later on in Khartoum he buys for Gerda a bottle of cognac because we could not buy this and he had his connections, you see!

Daily Affairs

I have found a house to my liking. The crate out of Holland has also arrived and can now be placed directly in the house. That will be a nice surprise for Gerda who is to arrive in Khartoum on 21 December '87. It is a very special day for Gerda, for the first time in Sudan, not directly the easiest country to get to know the tropics. We stay at the hotel Meridien and the next day we get on the road to Wad Medani. It is a dreary day with no sun and the fields along the road look empty and cheerless. Gerda is silent, she has a tiresome journey behind her and the travel in the Landover is not very pleasant. When we enter my room at the Gezira club I see her falter. I know what she is going through *"the blue period"* 'Ok' I say 'you are not going to do anything just now. Firstly you are going to lay on the bed, I make thee and then everything will be fine'!

After fifteen minutes Gerda is over the first culture shock. She gets up and I cannot stop her. Her suitcase is unpacked and all those good things out of the home country are displayed. That evening we eat by candle light and feel at home. My surprise for her is the house, which I have rented and the crate out of Holland with all our belongings which is stored there. The next afternoon after work we go to the house, unpack the crate and assemble the chairs. We have a nice Christmas with a service in Arabic in the Catholic church and a barbeque with the expatriate community on a little beach at the Nile. On the 12 January '88 Gerda departs for Holland but we want to continue with our relationship. Gerda likes to live in the tropics and Sudan. It is for her the answer to an old wish and which she now can bring to pass. The plan is; I shall take home leave in April and then we go back together to the Sudan.

Biologcal Control

It is the key word for the men of Wageningen. Dr. Joop v L. of the university and Barend B. of the FAO visit in March 1988. Joop is a passionate proponent of the control of harmful insects by means of predators and parasites. In fact he really does not like to use insecticides. In an experiment during the season 1986/87 Badar has demonstrated that natural enemies can play an important role to control harmful insects. This is a fact that the scientists and agricultural managers of the Sudan kind of have forgotten.

Assim, Badar and me make plans to introduce the parasitic wasp *Trichogramma sp.,* which lays its eggs in the eggs of the bollworm night butterfly (*Heliothis sp.*). Now the *Trichogramma* wasp measures no more than 1 mm and an egg of a *Heliothis sp.* has a diameter of about 2 mm. The plan is that following up my home leave in the Netherlands I collect the eggs at the university of Texas, America. Then, when travelling back to the Sudan, during a stopover at Schiphol airport, I hand over the packet of *Trichogramma* eggs to a co-worker of a bio-control company, which then will raise the wasps further. And that is the way it happens.

I fly to the Netherlands on 19 April '88 and there is the get together with Gerda and our two families. It is a time to relax and make social plans for the future and time flies. Then early May Gerda and I depart for the USA. First to Baton Rouge and then College Station, Texas. In Baton Rouge we stay with Joe and Anne and they immediately take to Gerda. Anne has her convictions. We are not married so we both get separate rooms. Gerda also meets Shelley and Marilyn, old friends of my student days and they like each other straight away. I visit my old department of Entomology and I experience the feeling of how small these corridors, rooms and laboratories are, where I spent so much time as a student. Dr. Larry R. is now the big boss of the LSU experimental station and he receives me with open arms. He draws me into that large office of his and says 'Piet this room is yours, use it and make yourself at home '. I meet other former teachers. We drink café and reminisce about the past. It is a pleasure to see and speak these men again.

I telephone with Dr. Maxwell, head of the department of Entomology of the university of Texas, College Station. We make an appointment for a meeting and for the collection of the *Trichogramma* eggs. We fly from Baton Rouge to Houston, where we rent a car and drive then to College Station, where we take a room in a motel. At the university I am cordially received by Dr. Maxwell and that evening he takes us out for dinner. He is very curious about what we intend to do in the Sudan. The next day I collect a packet of *Trichogramma* eggs and we drive back to Houston, where we take the plane to Schiphol.

It is our stop over on our way to the Sudan. In the arrival

hall I hand over the packet of *Trichogramma* eggs to the co-worker of the Biological firm, who is waiting for us. The first phase of the Bio-control project has been concluded satisfactorily. End September 1988 we receive the message that we can expect the first parcel with *Trichogramma* eggs.

An important occasion. Badar goes to Khartoum but returns empty handed. It appears that the importation of the wasps requires much paperwork and yes that is my department. It is an effort to finalize the import procedure in time, but we succeed. In October '88 the first *Trichogramma* wasps are released in cotton fields of the Rahad region. In the Gezira fields *Trichogramma's* are released during the seasons 1989/90 and 1990/91. The import procedure has then become a matter of practice.

Day to Day Affairs

Gerda leaves for Holland on 13 April '89, to get the house in order and to organize this and that before I come home on the 4th of May. However during the two intermediate weeks I get an attack of Malaria and I am really sick for one week. However with the use of the required medication I am recovered in time for my departure to the Netherlands. We have many plans for our holiday. One of the bungalows of Gerda comes free and we decide to live there. Her big house where she lived is just too cumbersome to maintain when we are away in the Sudan, so Gerda decides to sell it. The new house has to be fitted out. All my belongings have to be transferred from Deventer, where I had them stored with a logistics company. Also by brother Gerard I have to collect several suitcases. But first we want to go to Italy by motorcycle. However that is unexpectedly not possible. The motor is serviced, the route mapped out and the day before departure the BMW is parked completely packed in the garage, so that we can depart directly next day. That morning, 17 May 1989, I don't feel well when I get up. 'Let's postpone the travel for one day 'I say 'because I do not feel too good' and then I stay in bed the whole day. The next day I feel really sick. I have my suspicions and we go to the hospital in Vlissingen for a blood test. The result causes a small sensation there. Malaria is in the province Zeeland is hardly a household word. I inform the head office of the FAO and I am allowed two weeks sick leave. I am also requested to visit afterwards Rome for a week to discuss the Sudan program. There is progress with the organization of our new home. There is painting and repapering and a carpet is installed. A gas fire in the living room is connected and we buy some furniture. It is a special experience to unpack my suitcases and boxes after twenty years and to give all our belongings a place in our new home. For me it is a very special moment when we move into our new house, because it is the first time that I have my own permanent home in the Netherlands.

There are of course other matters which require my attention. A colleague of Wageningen has strongly suggested that I start making use of a computer. He himself started with this technology not too long ago and he is enthusiastic. Together with Gerda I buy my first computer in Rotterdam, 6 June 1989. It has a hard disk of 20 MB. It is quite an exercise because this science is completely new to me.

I am full of admiration when I see a young man working a computer. He types a few letters and then that machine is coming to life, amazing, how is this possible ! 'I think I should take that machine with two disk drives' I say hesitating. 'I still have to learn how to work this thing, so I don't need that more expensive computer'! The salesman is a professional, who cares about his customers and wants the best for them. He becomes emotional and his voice breaks when he almost begs me to please buy the machine with the hard disk. 'Sir, it is the future ' he says 'that computer with the two disk drives is the past'. I listen to his expert advice and buy the correct computer, a printer, cables and the WordPerfect program, strongly recommended by the colleague of Wageningen, as being the program which is used by everybody.

At home everything remains nicely packed. It is beyond me to start learning how to use it. One week before departure to Sudan, something has to be done. Rien, the man of sister in law Paula, instructor at a trade school, has followed courses in the use of computers, has become a fervent user, and is extremely helpful. Together with a colleague of his school my computer is made ready for use and during one afternoon they give me a short course in the use of the machine. When finished I am able to connect everything and to start WordPerfect. I am in business.

The Coup d'État

We fly to the Sudan, Wednesday, 28 June 1989. That Friday there is some big news. There has been a military coup and the government of Sadiq el Madi is no more. The colonel Omar el Bashir becomes the new president with as assistants several army officers. That evening the men appear on TV. The conceit is there to see. 'We are going to solve all the problems of Sudan' is the repeated exclamation, 'we know how to talk as one soldier to another with colonel Garang of the South'. The conflict between the North and the South has been going on for several years now and there did not seem to be soon a solution to the conflict. A new Minister of Agriculture is being appointed. He is a scientist of the ARC, a colleague who worked with vegetables and very important he is a proponent of IPM. Assim, Badar, Dr Osman and myself visit with him on 20 July at the Ministry of Agriculture, to congratulate him on his appointment. He is happy to see us, kind of nervous and has yet to get used to his new social standing. During later visits it is clear that he is now the Minister, although he remains for us the colleague with whom we can work together.

The Breakthrough

One afternoon, early July 1989, Dr Osman enters my office. With a little smile on his face he lets me know the request of the Minister; who likes to have a report on the present state of affairs of the research results on IPM. Now that is good news for us. This can be a breakthrough for the program when the politic shows interest for whatever reason. Dr Osman is kind of amazed, to formulate his reaction as such, when I inform him that an extensive report will be on the desk of the Minister at the end of the week.

The new government is based on the principles of the Islam and Sheria law. There has to come an end to intrigues and unnecessary wasting. The high costs for the use of insecticides has to be reduced significantly. Therefore the first matter of particular interest for the Minister is therefore to introduce IPM as soon as possible. All of a sudden our program gets attention and our recommendations are studied at length.

The meetings of the National Committee for Pests and Diseases are important. They are attended by scientists, managers of agricultural schemes and senior officials of the Ministry of Agriculture. Here the guidelines are determined for the use of pesticides in Sudan. Badar and myself are invited to attend the 25th meeting of the Committee, which shall take place on 15 August 1989. I notice that several officials of the Ministry have received their instructions.

It is decided that IPM techniques shall be used on a trial

basis on a large scale in the Gezira and Rahad regions. The ETL's shall be increased according to our recommendations in each region for 2000 ha during the 1989/90 season. It is also decided that this experiment shall be implemented as a commercial undertaking and shall be executed by the managements of the two schemes. This means that the fields will be sampled each week by their field workers. The IPM team shall however also sample the respective fields weekly. Decisions with regard to the use of insecticides shall be made jointly. That is the way it happens.

August '89 the fields are sown in. Assim, Badar and myself have a meeting in the office of Badar. With regard to the results of the past seasons we determine the ETL's to be used for the different insect pests. There is a good discussion. The ETL's can be raised a good deal, in that we are in agreement, but we have to decide how far. I am too optimistic, Badar too careful and then with Assim as mediator we come to the right decision. This is important, if this demonstration succeeds we have a breakthrough and IPM can become the plant protection philosophy for cotton cultivation in the Sudan. (5)

Te following months are busy with visitors from the World bank and the university of Wageningen. Yes, also the World bank is involved in this Endeavour, because if the yields in the IPM demonstration areas would be considerable lower than expected, then the respective farmers shall receive a compensation, funded by the World bank. Without this guarantee, it would have been very difficult to obtain their cooperation.

There is the routine of fieldwork, the meetings and all the day to day logistics, which come with a project of this size. Often I am not able to visit the fields every week with the boys. Then there is the day of truth, the cotton harvest is there. It is February 1990 and a large delegation, which consists of senior managers of the production areas, scientists and senior co-workers of the Ministry of Agriculture shall visit the IPM demonstration fields. Such excursions of the senior agricultural people take place once or twice each season. They are always festive occasions, with much to eat and drink and with once in a while a little walk in a cotton field.

This field visit has a special dimension; the expected yields and pest infestations in the IPM fields. We are on the way, it is a very long row of land cruisers, which moves through the fields. There is a kind of special tension, the expectation of something particular, the solution of a long standing controversy. There are suddenly rumors that the harvest results in the respective fields are not too good. People are already looking for a scapegoat. I am being avoided, people do not want to associate with me. I relax myself. I have done the utmost, taking risks, giving trust to co-workers, now I have to hand over and accept what has to be and don't get excited. The caravan stops near the first IPM field. Everybody scrambles out of the cars and runs into the field. Plants are examined, cotton lint is felt and then there are amazed looks and exclamations. The plants look beautiful and it promises to be a very good harvest. The general mood changes completely when also the other fields show similar promise. I have kept myself apart, but now everybody approaches me and the IPM team is congratulated with this exceptional result. I look up and say silently "*thank you*", because to experience such a result is very special. IPM has proven itself.

A Marriage and Other Affairs

It is March 1990 when I ask Gerda if she wants to marry me. We have been together now for three years and that is enough time for her to know that she wants to continue with this man. So she says yes and we celebrate this very important occasion with several friends and a telegram to the family. 'I think they will be very happy' I laugh 'Gerda again a respectable woman and Pieter again tied to an apron'. The colleagues think it the correct commitment to make. Social contacts become easier and that makes life for an International civil servant somewhat more straightforward. On the 26 April we land at Schiphol for a holiday period and on 25 May 1990 we marry in the church of Kleverskerke in the presence of family and a few good friends, it is a festive occasion. With all those sisters and brothers and their children of Gerda I have now gained an extensive family. It requires study and improvisation to remember all those names and when I forget to give new ones. And then there are the new acquaintances in Arnemuiden, because Gerda is well known in this village. So that first year I remain there "that man of our Gerda" and I don't count.

As regard to work, the year 1990 is not an easy one for me. I am not directly a diplomat and when I am convinced that my vision is correct than it can happen that I have no patience with some ego's in the head office. And yes, that attitude can cause problems and you make it yourself not easy that way. Therefore Gerda and I take 10 days leave in the Netherlands in December that year, just to relax after this past strenuous period, so that we can start afresh in January 1991. In the meantime something is happening in the Middle East. The Persian Gulf war started in August '90, with the invasion of Kuwait by the Iraqi army. There is a real possibility that the Americans, at the head of an International coalition of 34 countries shall invade Iraq. We depart again for the Sudan on 4 January 1991. It is known that the present rulers of Sudan are in support of Iraq, but when we arrive in Khartoum we do not experience a negative attitude, Daily life goes on as usual. There is a positive reaction of one of the colleagues when I enter a few days later the compound of the ARC. He is hardly a proponent of IPM, quite the contrary generally,since insecticides are his "bread and butter" so to speak. However he greats me heartily and puts up his thumb. This is a nice home coming, to experience that somehow you are respected and appreciated.

However the International community does not feel at ease with regard to the Gulf war and the possibility that Sudan gets actively involved. Much UN personnel departs for Kenya or other neighboring countries, because the reasoning is; everything is possible. However I am determined to stay on in Sudan because my work here is not finished yet. We are on the brink of a breakthrough and therefore I am happy when my contract is extended for one more year.

Training

Achmed el S., our extension specialist is a very sincere and active colleague. He is an American, originally from Irak and has experienced difficult times. He organizes information days with banners, slide presentations and briefings with scientists. Of course there are always the necessary consumptions and drinks (no my good reader, no alcohol). It is always a still pleasure for me to see Achmed at work. He is the organizer and walks to and fro with a frown on his face, says a few words here, signs with his arms there and can then whisper gravely to me some suggestion or instruction, which I then do not understand! Yes Achmed is a very good man and an asset to the project. In a period of two years there have been 80 meetings, during which the message of IPM has been proclaimed to farmers, agricultural teachers, women groups, students and agricultural managers.

A Disappointment

There has been a symposium on IPM in the large conference hall of the ARC. The podium is still decorated with of banners, describing the many advantages of applying IPM. A large meeting for the entire ARC staff has been scheduled and we of the IPM team have also been invited.. Dr N. Burlough, the Nobel prize winner, the man of the green revolution, is visiting the Sudan and shall address the congregation. Well his presentation is for the IPM team a great disappointment. The good man, ok, and much respect here, talks for one hour and is of the opinion that one should use insecticides. He points to a IPM banner; very good, but please do not excluded chemicals. The room is all ears and yes there are covered looks my direction. I use my head, keep my temper and do not say a word. When the meeting is over there is a moment of getting together and there is time for a brief talk. 'Oh yes, IPM is a very good policy for a responsible way to implement insect pest control. Oh damn, I would have liked if he would have stressed this point during his address, instead of putting emphasis on the use of insecticides.

Computers

Even in Sudan computers are getting to be important. The men of Wageningen advice that we should organize a computer course and that is going to happen. Dr Lukas N. a young enthusiastic scientist, arrives in Kartoum in January '89 with a real big portable computer on his back. He also brought a bottle of Sambuca spirit, he tells me but the custom official made him throw it away through the toilet. In the meantime our project computer has arrived and is now being installed and programmed by Lukas. He also gives a training for the IPM team and administrative staff. Lukas is young, very smart, a computer wizard and who can also work very hard. He shall go far. In May '90 he is back and then he conducts a three week computer course for the scientists of the ARC.

Training abroad

An academic training abroad for young promising ARC scientists is considered top priority In our budget we have funds to finance the further education abroad for seven students. Geneed H. is a young assistant in the IPM program, with the silent wish to become a famous scientist. In the field he likes to walk around in a white laboratory frock and then gives important instructions to the field staff. He also has his connections and one day Dr Osman, the director general of the ARC, enters my office for a nice little chat. He and the colleagues are of the opinion that Geneed is an excellent candidate for a PhD study in America and yes I have understood the point. Badar and myself are not directly convinced of this fact but we cannot ignore the wishes of the national colleagues.

There is a visit of a professor of a university in America. He is looking for suitable candidates for his Faculty of Entomology. There is a talk together with Badar. And then there is the carnal question; what we think of candidate Geneed. Badar and myself look at each other briefly and then say together that Geneed is a nice young man who should have a chance to prove himself. The professor is satisfied and Badar and myself feel ourselves a little holy now that we have not ruined the future of a young man.

Materials

During a period of three years quite a number of articles

have been ordered under which two Toyota land cruisers, which arrive mid 1989. Until then we only had a Peugeot station wagon and a Toyota pickup truck, which were kept running with much ingenuity and effort. The arrival of the two land cruisers is a very important happening to which we have been looking forward to with much anticipation. There are some tense moments when the two cars are being unloaded from a special truck, with the help of a derelict crane and chains. There is some damage to paint and bodywork, but that is under Sudan conditions of no importance. I design a service roster for all the cars and a logbook for each car in which the driver has to keep a record of travel and maintenance. The cars are important to the program, because without reliable transport we cannot do our work efficiently. To store all our materials safely I buy two large sea containers, which are being placed on the ARC compound. The keys are in a drawer of the desk in my office and only the immediate co-workers are familiar where the keys are stored. Besides our driver Sheggah, already years with the program, we have engaged a second driver.

Yusuf is of origin Ugandese and has arrived along a certain way in Sudan. He seems on first impression a very nice and gentle person. But there is another Yusuf. One morning, in Khartoum, on the way home, an old woman crosses the road. In the blink of an eye Yusuf's friendly face sports a grin of malicious joy when he brakes the car just in front of her, what causes a frightened reaction of her. My reaction is not mentioned here, because sometimes I am somewhat vehement when I get upset.

One day I arrive at the office at 8.00 o'clock in the morning. Osman, my administrative assistant, is already present and is kind of upset. The doors of the containers are wide open and many of the goods have been stolen. Damn, damn,

I am furious, how can this be possible. Somebody must have taken the keys from my desk drawer. There is a police investigation and already soon the culprit is known. Most of the articles are found in the house of Yusuf. Darn, I feel really bad and disappointed. When a policeman passes by my office for a statement the next morning, I see that his right hand is bandaged. I have a suspicion how this injury came about, however I cannot feel compassion for the man, who received the punishment.

The Results of Hard Work

It will be a close call. The 57th yearly meeting of the National Pests and Diseases Committee is scheduled to take place for 3 July 1991. With regard to the results of the last three years we have made the following recommendation; to increase the ETL's for bollworm, whitefly, jassid and aphid on cotton. We are of the opinion that there is a good chance that our recommendations will be accepted, because it has been demonstrated many times that with these increased ETL's very good yields have been realized with lower production costs. We also know that the Ministry of Agriculture is a great proponent to increase the ETL's, since it reduces the high costs for insecticides used on cotton. However we do not take anything for granted because we know there is much opposition to be expected from the "Insecticide lobby".

The big day is there, and the large conference room of the ARC, where the meeting shall take place, is crowded. Anybody of importance is present. There is right from the start a tense atmosphere and I realize that the opponents of IPM have been busy. One after the other proponents of the preventive use of insecticides present their case. Assim, Badar and myself are utterly disappointed, when Dr Hassan B., a young scientist and a co-worker of the IPM team, suddenly, and completely unexpected speaks out against IPM. It is a knife in the back. The young man has been persuaded by some of his senior colleagues.

It has now become a game of words, where scientific data are suddenly not important anymore. Some smart numbers call that Dr Stam should speak, but I know better. I request Assim, the National director of the IPM program to state our point of view. Assim is a very good speaker and he knows whom he 's dealing with. Systematically he refutes the arguments of the opponents and refers to the excellent harvest results, the improved quality of the cotton lint and the reduced production costs. We get the support of the senior representatives of the Ministry of Agriculture and the senior managers of the Gezira and Rahad schemes.

There is a vote and it is decided to increase the ETL's for the bollworm and the whitefly to the recommended levels. However for the jassid and the aphid the proposed ETL's are rejected. It is felt that more data are needed and that these proposals shall be discussed during the next yearly meeting. Then the meeting is closed.

Assim is outraged that Hassan has turned around. He is also angry with some of his colleagues of whom he feels that they have opposed him out of spite. He stays to talk after the meeting. Badar and I walk to his office, we are both drained and tired from the tension of the past emotional hours. Badar makes thee.

At first there is disappointment that the ETL's for jassids and aphids have been rejected. But then slowly there is the realization that with the result for the two most important insect pests, the bollworm and the whitefly, we have achieved a result which is really trail blazing in the history of crop protection in the Sudan. Suddenly there is euphoria that we have reached this result after so many years of hard work and disappointments. When Assim enters, still angry, he soon shares in the rejoicing and there is laughter and we look back on what has happened in the past. Starting out we could not have anticipated that this would be the results of four years of work. Our predecessors could certainly not have expected that IPM would be accepted in the Sudan. Especially in the beginning everything looked kind of hopeless. The chemical lobby was powerful and well represented and it sponsored research. The IPM program on the contrary, had not much to offer financially. There came a change in attitude when the political landscape changed. The new rulers realized that the production costs for the very important cotton industry were not realistic and that the use of expensive insecticides should be reduced drastically. Especially for Assim, after working for twelve years on IPM, the recent results are a very special occasion. But also Badar and I feel privileged as well to be part and parcel to this landmark in plant protection on cotton.

The Last Episode

My work in Sudan has come to an end. I feel that I have to finish my period in the Sudan now that the main goal has been reached. However, before we are going to leave Sudan there is still much to do. During the period; June '91 untill January '92 there are regular meetings with farmers and other interested parties, during which the new ETL's are discussed and explained. There are several evaluation missions and much time is spend with the preparations for the construction of the new IPM building. A design is approved in October '91 and a contract is being signed by a builder in January '92.

There is an impressive farewell dinner with all the colleagues of the ARC and the production schemes present. I say goodbye to all those people with whom I have worked so closely during these past years. Dr Osman, who has now a very profitable position with a Japanese chemical company, looks amazed when I come to take leave of him. I notice that he really appreciates my gesture to come and shake his hand. In Khartoum the FAO representative throws a huge party for Gerda and me and then we depart for Egypt for a two week holiday. Then it is off to Rome where I shall write at FAO headquarters my "end of mission "report and to finalize my personnel logistics.

Holiday in Egypt

We have planned our stay in Egypt well. The first week we shall travel on our own and then the second week we have booked a travel holiday with a Dutch agency with which we shall connect in Cairo. Through a travel agent in Khartoum we book accommodation in Cairo for the first week and we also receive the address of a dependable taxi service, as being assured. Well we will see! When we arrive in Cairo our taxi driver is already waiting for us, who introduces himself as Ali B. A little trade about costs and then he shall be our guide for the coming week. Ali appears to be a very pleasant companion. Under his guidance we explore Cairo, visit the market (souk)where haggling about prices is great sport, equally enjoyed and appreciated by the traders. We also visit Alexandria and its harbor.

Then the second week we transfer to a first class hotel where we meet our fellow travelers out of the Netherlands, for a Nile cruise. We shake hands, try to remember names and then it is getting into a bus that will bring us to some location for a cup of coffee and lunch. We are in luck with this group of people. After one hour the atmosphere is very relaxed and we are all on first name basis. It is for us the first time that we participate in an organized group travel. We did not expect that it would be so much fun. We make a beautiful tour over the Nile and there is no worry about the travel logistics and hotel reservations. Everything has been taken care of and that is getting used to but also very relaxing.

Rome and the end

This time around, Rome is a very special and nice experience. Mother has always been very curious and energetic and loves to travel. She came up with the idea to meet her son and his wife in Rome and then together have a nice little holiday. Well that is an excellent idea and also father and mother Poortvliet like to visit. Then sister Paula and husband Rien also like to come along. It is very nice to have the whole family together in the dining room of the hotel. During the day the family visit the town and I work at the head office. I write my end of mission report, finalize the project administration and accounts and organize my personal logistics. Early April 1992 we are home again. An important period in our lives has come to an end.

Pieter Stam

Sudan, put Trichogramma out in the field

Sudan, field visit

Sudan, cotton harvest

Work with setbacks in Uganda (1992)

The beginning

In June 1992 I receive an enquiry by telephone from IFAD (*International Fund for Agricultural Development*), if I am available for a consultancy in Uganda. The World bank is carrying out a feasibility a study to finance a Smallholder Crop Diversification Pilot Project (SCDPP) in Uganda. IFAD has been requested to deliver an expert, who can prepare a project proposal for a IPM program for small scale cotton growing with attention for the environment. There is the request if I can be present in the IFAD office in Rome for instruction and if I can then depart for Uganda as quickly as possible to meet with the team of the World bank. They are in a hurry.

The invitation comes at a somewhat inconvenient time. I am not yet entirely rested from the exertions in Sudan. I request that I start one week later, but I shall regret this delay. It is also a hard lesson. When, as an independent consultant, you are offered a contract, don't deliberate but be positive immediately. If you hesitate you will lose the work or you will not have enough time to carry out the assignment, because your new employer is often too late to start the program.

In the IFAD office I meet Henk G., the man who has engaged me, and there is an immediate rapport. There is the necessary paperwork to do; signing of contract, the cognizance of the objectives of the work in Uganda and to study the background of the World bank project concerned. On 6 July I fly via Athene, Addis Abeba, to Entebe Uganda.

Day to day affairs

Sometimes you have those periods in life when everything works against you; you make the wrong choices, there are unnecessary conflict situations and you ask yourself, how did I get into this mess. When I arrive in Uganda I learn that my colleagues, the consultants of the World bank, have already left to the North of Uganda. In the office of the World bank in Kampala I find out where they are and I am forced to close up with them on my own. I have some experience with travelling in Africa and I have not too much luggage with me and easy to carry, so I am well prepared for this travel. At the bus station, in dust and heath, I find after asking and pushing a seat in a crowded little bus. Jammed in like a sardine in a tin, we bump along rural dusty roads to the place of destination. That evening I enter the hotel where the team is staying. The welcome by my colleagues is not directly enthusiastic. 'We had not counted on you being a member of this evaluation mission 'says the team leader, a national of Nigeria in permanent employment of the World bank. 'The IPM module could have been done by Dr. Ken B., the plant breeder'. Dr. Ken earnestly confirms that he could do this work. Well I am not so convinced about his expertise on IPM, but I explain that I am engaged by IFAD to prepare an IPM program as part of the World bank project and that, as far as I know, is all there is to it. My explanation is sufficient and there is no more talk about it. I am accepted as a member of the team. For the next two weeks much work is being done and I get to know the colleagues, who know each other from other World bank missions.

The work program

Cotton in Uganda is rain fed and cultivated mainly by small scale farmers, who grow also food crops, which include maize, finger millet, rice, beans, ground nuts, banana's and cassava. A typical farmer might cultivate 1-2 ha, on which he grows his cash and food crops in a rotational system. The fields will be surrounded by elephant grass. Some farmers work closely together and have organized themselves in collectives. Cotton is usually the opening crop after fallow. It requires intensive weeding, which ensures that the land needs less labor input for the following cereal crops. Land preparation: This starts in most cases with bush clearing, which is done by hand, after which the land is hoed by hand or ploughed by oxen or tractor. Planting dates vary between early May to mid-August, depending on the rains, available labor (competition of food crops)) and inputs (seed, credits etc). Planting is done by hand. Harvesting is also carried out by hand, often in three pickings.

Last day to day affairs

Back in Kampala I have a traumatic experience; in that US$ 3000,- in traveler cheques are being stolen. This is really very inconvenient. It is quite an exercise to organize money for my further stay. Back in the Netherlands it takes about three months and several telephone conversations with the head office of the travel cheque bank in New York, before I get a refund for the money lost.

Back in Rome there awaits a last ordeal. At the office I write my end of mission report. The director of IFAD, an Egyptian, was not present when I first arrived at the office but now he wants to meet with me and I am introduced to him by Henk. The meeting is not a success. There is from the beginning a mutual feeling of antipathy. The man treads me as a subordinate and there is an argument. I am sometimes rather sensitive in such situations and that is not advisable. Just keep on smiling, do not take notice of impolite and rude behavior of persons, who own their positions due to political influence. Easily said, but sometimes it is too much. When my report is finished and accepted I say goodbye to Henk and another Dutchman, whom I have met in the office and I return home. It has been an educative experience.

Bibliography

1) Stam, P.A., D.F. Clower, J.B. Graves, and P.E. Schilling. 1978. Effects of certain herbicides on some insects and spiders found in Louisiana cotton fields. J. Econ. Entomol. 71:477-480.

2) Stam, P.A., L.D. Newsom, and E.N. Lambremont. 1987. Predation and food as factors affecting survival of Nezara viridula (L.) (Hemiptera: Pentatomidae) in a soybean ecosystem.Environ. Entomol. 16:1211-1216.

3) Stam, P.A. 1987. Creotiades pallidus (R.) (Hemiptera, Miridae), a pest on cotton along the Euphrates river and its effect on yield and control action threshold in the Syrian Arab Republic. Trop. Pest Managm. 33:273-276.

4) Stam, P.A. and H. Elmosa. 1990. The role of predators and parasites in controlling populations of Earias insulana, Heliothis armigera, and Bemisia tabaci on cotton in the Syrian Arab Republic. Entomophaga 35:315-327.

5) Stam, P.A., A.A. Abdelrahman and B. Munir. 1994. Comparisons of control action thresholds for Heliothis armigera, Bemisia tabaci and Aphis gossypii on cotton in the Sudan Gezira and Rahad regions. Crop Protection 13:503-512.

6) Lambremont, E.N., F.A. Iddings, P.A. Stam, and R.B. Sgrillo. 1977. A method for in vivo counting of radiophosphorus in insects by detection of cerenkov radiation in water. Ann. Entomol. Soc. Amer. 70:757-760.

7) Kalroo, A.M., P.A. Stam, and A.A. Baloch. 1993. The spotted bollworm damage to cotton in Sindh. Modern Agriculture 4:12-15

8) Buriro, A.S. and P.A. Stam. 1995. Integrated Pest Management in Cotton. Sampling Harmful and Beneficial Insects. IPM Research Dir.Gen.Agric. Res. Sindh, Pakistan. 16 p. Field manual; a pictorial guide of insects.

Printed in the United States
By Bookmasters